To Jennifer with our love —
Uncle Mike
Aunt Jo
Christmas 1990

$3.50

THE MANGER IS EMPTY

THE MANGER IS EMPTY

STORIES IN TIME

WALTER WANGERIN, JR.

1817

Harper & Row, Publishers, San Francisco

New York, Grand Rapids, Philadelphia, St. Louis
London, Singapore, Sydney, Tokyo, Toronto

Library of Congress Cataloging-in-Publication Data

Wangerin, Walter.
    The manger is empty : stories in time / Walter Wangerin, Jr.—
1st ed.
        p.   cm.
    ISBN 0-06-061180-4 :
    I. Title.
PS3573.A477M36   1989
242—dc20   89-45237
                                                        CIP

89 90 91 92 93 HAD 10 9 8 7 6 5 4 3 2

For Susan,
kin to me and very kind

Contents

CHRISTMAS:
The Season in White

1. The Manger Is Empty

My daughter cried on Christmas Eve. What should I say to the heart of my daughter? How should I comfort her?

Her name is Mary. She's a child. She wasn't crying the tears of disillusionment, as adults do when they've lost the spirit of the season. And she trusts me. I do not lie. My Mary is easily able to throw her arms around me in the kitchen and to hang on with a hug—proving that she trusts me. Neither, then, was she weeping the tears of an oversold imagination that Christmas Eve. She hadn't dreamed a gift too beautiful to be real, nor had she expected my love to buy better than my purse.

Nor was she sick. Nor was she hungry for any physical thing.

No, Mary was longing for Odessa Williams, that old black lady. Mary was longing for her life. That's why she was crying.

Too suddenly the child had come to the limits of the universe. A casket. She stood at the edge of emptiness and had no other response than tears. She turned to me and wept against my breast, and I am her father. And should I be mute before such tears? What should I say to the heart of my daughter Mary?

We have a custom in our congregation: always we gather on the Sunday evening before Christmas, bundled and hatted and happy, and we go, then, out into the sharp December darkness to sing carols. Down the streets of the city we go, the children bounding forward, adults all striding behind, chattering, making congenial noises, puffing ghosts of breath beneath the streetlights, laughing and glad for the company. Does anyone think it will snow? It's cold enough to snow, and the air is still, and the stars are already a snow-dust in heaven.

It's a common, communal custom. You do it too?

We crowd on the porches of the old folks. The children feel a squealing excitement because they think we're about to astonish Mrs. Moody in her parlor by our sudden appearing— carols from the out-of-doors, you know. She'll be so-o-o-o surprised! So they giggle and roar a marvelous *Hark!* with their faces pressed against her window: *Hark! The herald angels sing, glory to the newborn king—*

Mrs. Moody turns on her porch light, then opens her curtains, and there she is, shaking her head and smiling, and the children fairly burst with glee. They can hardly stand it, to be so good. She turns on her porch light, and here we are, fifteen, maybe twenty of us, spilling down her steps into the little yard, lifting our faces, lifting our voices—doing silly things, like lifting our key-rings to the refrain of "Jingle Bells" and making a perfect, rhythmic jangle. Everybody's willing to be a kid. Nobody minds the cold tonight. The white faces among us are pinched with pink; the black ones (we are mostly black ones) frost, as though the cold were a white dust on our cheeks.

And down the street we go again, and so we sing for Mrs. Lander and Mrs. Smith and Mrs. Buckman and Mrs. DeWitt.

And though we can be silly, and though this is just an ordinary custom, yet we are no ordinary choir. No: many of us sing for "The Sounds of Grace," a choir of legitimate repute. And some of us have been blessed by God with voices the angels would weep to own.

For sometimes on that Sunday evening, by a decision that no one understands, Timmy Moore will begin a solo in a husky and generous tenor voice. *O holy night,* the young man starts to sing, and then we are all an audience, listening in a starry dark. *It is the night of the dear Savior's birth. Long lay the world,* sings Timmy Moore. We bow our heads. Mrs. DeWitt, on the inside of her window, bows her head. We are more than an audience. We are passengers. This strong voice is a sort of chariot, you know, able to carry us out of the streets of the city, through dark night, to the fields of shepherds far away. *Fall on your knees,* sings Timmy Moore, huge and strong, transported: *O hear the angel voices! O night divine! O night when Christ was born.* There is locomotive power in this, and truth, and utter conviction, and we can scarcely breathe. *O night! O night divine.*

So then, Timmy is silent. And what then? Why, then we all sing "Silent Night." And then occurs such a sweet and delicate wonder that Mrs. DeWitt looks up with the astonishment that the children had expected at first, but which none of the children notice now, for they are caught in the wonder too. Mrs. DeWitt looks up and starts to cry. She covers her mouth with an aged hand, and she cries.

For on the third verse of "Silent Night," Dee Dee Lawrence, that blinking, innocent child, soars high and high above us all on a descant so beautiful it can break your heart. Dee Dee simply flies, high and light, precise, to the stars themselves, to the crystal sphere of heaven, and we are singing too, but we have forgotten we sing. Dee Dee is the winter's bird, singing: *Son of God, love's pure light, Radiant beams from thy holy face—* And when that child has reached the crystal sphere, with the wing of her music she touches it, and all the round sky rings. The night is alive. This is the wonder that catches us all. *With the dawn of redeeming grace,* sings Dee Dee Lawrence, and then she sinks to the earth again: *Jesus, Lord, at thy birth,* descending, descending—innocent, I think, of the thing she has just accomplished—finding her place in the midst of earthly voices again. *Jesus, Lord, at thy birth.* And she is done. And we are done. We move in quietness to the next house.

Dee Dee Lawrence has a round, milk-chocolate face and an oriental cast to her eyes. Her beauty is not remarkable. Until she sings.

As we walk to the next house, we become aware that we, with Mrs. DeWitt, have been crying. That's why we are quiet. The tears are icy on our cheeks.

But these are good, contemplative tears. They are not like the tears my Mary cried on Christmas Eve.

And so it was that on Sunday evening, the twentieth of December, 1981, we kept our custom and went out caroling. Mary was seven years old then. Dee Dee was eight. Timmy was with us, and the Hildreth children. Most of the children's choir, in fact, had come along. The night was not much different from those that went before—except for this, that when we had finished our round of houses we went to St. Mary's Hospital to sing for several members who were patients at Christmas time. We divided into three groups. As pastor, I myself led a handful of children to the room of Odessa Williams because her condition was worse than the others.

It was Odessa Williams who made the night different.

The children had never laid eyes on her before. When they crept into the ward and saw her cadaverous body, they were speechless for a while. Scared, I think. Mary's blue eyes grew very large, and I felt pity for her.

Well, I knew what to expect, but Mary didn't. I had been visiting the woman for several years now—first in her apartment, where she'd been housebound, then in the nursing home—and I had watched the wasting of Odessa.

Two years ago she had been a strapping tall woman of strong ways, strong opinions, and very strong affections. Fiercely she had loved the church that she couldn't actually attend. She'd kept abreast of congregational activities by telephone, by a gossip-system, by bulletins and newsletters and friends—and by me. She pumped me for information every time I visited her, puffing an endless chain of cigarettes, striding about her apartment in crushed slippers, waving her old black arms in strong declaration of the things she thought I ought to do and the things I ought not, as pastor, to be doing.

I had learned, for my own protection, to check her mouth as soon as I entered her room. If the woman wore dentures, she was mad: she wanted her words to click with clarity, to snap and hiss with a precision equal to her anger. Mad at me, she needed teeth. But if she smiled a toothless smile on me, then I knew that her language would be soft and I had her approval—that week. She was particularly fierce regarding her children, the choir, the "Sounds of Grace," though she had never heard them sing. She loved them. She swelled with a grand, maternal love for them. And if ever I had not, by her estimate, done right by these children, the teeth in the mouth of Odessa Williams were the flashing, clacking weapons of an avenging angel.

It will be understood why I was never able to persuade the woman to stop smoking. Even in the nursing home she continued to smoke. But the disease that kept her housebound and sent her to the nursing home was cancer.

Cancer, finally, had laid her in the hospital.

And it was cancer that frightened the children when they crept around her bed on Sunday night, coming to sing carols to her. It put the odor of warm rot in the air. It had wasted Odessa to bone.

Mary and Dee Dee and Timmy and the others tried to touch nothing in the little space, not the bed, not the wall behind them. They grew solemn, unable to take their eyes from the form before them. One little lamp shed an orange light on the hollows of Odessa's face, sunken cheeks and sunken temples and deep, deep eyes. The lids on her eyes were thin as onion skin, half-closed; and her flesh was dry like parchment; and the body that once was strapping now resembled broomsticks in her bed—skinny arms on a caven stomach, fingers as long as chalk. And who could tell if the woman was breathing?

Mary stood across the bed from me, not looking at me, gazing down at Odessa. Mary's eyes kept growing larger.

So I whispered to all of them, "Sing." But they shuffled instead.

"What's this?" I whispered. "Did you lose your voices? Do you think she won't like it?"

"We think she won't hear," said Mary.

"No, no, sing the same as you always do," I said. "Sing for Miz Williams."

Well, and so they did, that wide-eyed ring of children, though it was a pitiful effort at first. "Away in a Manger," like nursery kids suspicious of their audience. But by the time the cattle were lowing, the children had found comfort in the sound of their own voices and began to relax. Moreover, Odessa had opened her eyes, and there was light in there, and she had begun to pick out their faces, and I saw that Mary was returning Odessa's look with a fleeting little smile. So then they harked it with herald angels, and they found in their bosoms a first noel that other angels did say, and then a marvelous thing began to happen: Odessa Williams was frowning—frowning and nodding, frowning with her eyes squeezed shut, frowning, you see, with fierce pleasure, as though she were chewing a delicious piece of meat. So then Mary and all the children were grinning, because they knew instinctively what the frown of an old black woman meant.

Odessa did not have her dentures in.

And the marvelous thing that had begun could only grow more marvelous still.

For I whispered, "Dee Dee," and the innocent child glanced at me, and I said, "Dee Dee, 'Silent Night.' "

Dear Dee Dee! That girl, as dark as the shadows around her, stroked the very air as though it were a chime of glass. (Dee Dee, I love you!) So high she soared on her crystal voice, so long she held the notes, that the rest of the children hummed and harmonized all unconsciously, and they began to sway together. "Round yon virgin, mother and child. . . ."

Odessa's eyes flew open to see the thing that was happening around her. She looked, then she raised her long, long arms; and then lying on her back, the old woman began to direct the music. By strong strokes she lifted Dee Dee Lawrence. She pointed the way, and Dee Dee trusted her, so Dee Dee sang a soprano descant higher and braver than she had ever sung before. Impossible! Stroke for stroke with imperious arms,

Odessa Williams gathered all her children and urged them to fly, and sent them on a celestial flight to glory, oh! These were not children anymore. These were the stars. Their voices ascended on fountains of light to become the very hosts of heaven—so high, so bright and holy and high. *Jesus, Lord, at thy birth!* So beautiful.

And then that woman brought them down again, by meek degrees to the earth again, and to this room and to her bedside; and there they stood, perfectly still, smiling in silence and waiting. How could anyone move immediately after such a wonder?

Nor did Odessa disappoint them. For then she began, in a low and smoky voice, to preach.

"Oh, children—you my choir," Odessa whispered. "Oh, choir—you my children for sure. An' listen me," she whispered intently. She caught them one by one on the barb of her eye. "Ain' no one stand in front of you for goodness, no! You the bes', babies. You the absolute *best.*"

The children gazed at her, and the children believed her completely: they were the best. And my Mary, too, believed what she was hearing, heart and soul.

"Listen me," Odessa said. "When you sing, wherever you go to sing, look down to the front row of the people who come to hear you sing. There's alluz an empty seat there. See it?" The children nodded. They saw it. "Know what that empty space is?" The children shook their heads. "It's me," she said, and they nodded. "It's me," she whispered in the deep orange light. "'Cause I alluz been with you, children. An' whenever you sing, I'm goin' to be with you still. An' you know how I can say such a mackulous thing?" They waited to know. She lowered her voice, and she told them. "Why, 'cause we in Jesus," she whispered the mystery. "Babies, babies, we be in the hand of Jesus, old ones, young ones, and us and you together. Jesus, he hold us in his hand, and ain' no one goin' to snatch us out. Jesus, he don' never let one of us go. Never. Not ever—"

So spoke Odessa, and then she fell silent. So said the woman with such conviction and such fierce love, that the children rolled tears from their open eyes, and they were not ashamed. They reached over and patted the bones of her body beneath the blankets.

Mary's eyes too were glistening. The woman had won my daughter. In that incandescent moment, Mary had come to love Odessa Williams. She slipped her soft hand toward the bed and touched the tips of Odessa's fingers, and she smiled and cried at once. For this is the power of a wise love wisely expressed: to transfigure a heart, suddenly, forever.

But neither were these like the tears that Mary wept on Christmas Eve.

2.

On Tuesday, the twenty-second of December, Odessa Williams died.

It had been a long time coming, but was quick when it came. She died in her sleep and went to God without her dentures.

Quick when it came, I say: Odessa left us little time to mourn for her. Gaines Funeral Home had less than a day to prepare her body, because the wake would take place on Wednesday evening. The funeral itself had to be scheduled for Thursday morning. There was no alternative. Friday was Christmas Day; Saturday and Sunday were the weekend; Gaines would be closed for three days straight, and Monday was too far away to make Odessa wait for burial. She would be buried, then, on Christmas Eve Day.

And I, for my own part, was terribly distracted by a hectic week. This was the very crush of the season, you see, with a children's pageant and extra services to prepare. My pastoral duty was already doubled; Odessa's funeral tripled it. So I rushed from labor to labor, more pastor than father, more worker than wise.

Not brutally, but somewhat busily at lunch on Wednesday,

I mentioned to my children that Miz Williams had died. They were eating soup. This was not an unusual piece of news in our household: the congregation had its share of elderly.

I scarcely noticed, then, that Mary stopped eating and stared at her bowl of soup.

I wiped my mouth and rose from the table.

"Dad?"

I was trying to remember what time the children should be at church to rehearse the Christmas program. Timing was everything. I wanted to give them a last instruction before I left.

"Dad?"

One thirty! "Listen—Mom will drive you to church at one fifteen. Can you all be ready then?"

"Dad?"

"Mary, what?" She was still staring at the soup, large eyes lost behind her hair.

"Is it going to snow tomorrow?" she said.

"What? I don't know. How would I know that?"

"It shouldn't snow," she said.

"You always wanted snow at Christmas."

In a tiny voice she whispered, "I want to go to the funeral."

Well, then that was it: she was considering what to wear against the weather. I said, "Fine," and left.

Thursday came grey and hard and cold and windless. It grudged the earth a little light and made no shadow. The sky was sullen, draining color from the grass and the naked trees. I walked to church in the morning.

We have a custom in our congregation: always, before a funeral service begins, we set the casket immediately in front of the chancel and leave it open about an hour. People come for a final viewing of the body, friends who couldn't attend the wake, acquaintances on their way to work, strangers out of the past, memories, stories that will never be told. The dead one lies the same for all who gaze at her, infinitely patient. So people enter the church, and they creep up the aisle, and they look, and they think, and they leave again.

Soon some of the mourners remain. They keep their coats on, but they sit in the pews and wait. They remind me of winter birds on telephone wires, their plumage all puffed around them, their faces closed, contemplative.

And then, ten minutes before the service, I robe myself and stand in the back of the church to meet the greater flow of mourners. Last of all the family will arrive in limousines. I keep peeping out of the door to see whether the silent cars have slid to their places at the curb—

And so it was that on Christmas Eve at eleven in the morning I discovered Mary outside the door. In fact, she was standing on the sidewalk while her mother parked the car. She was staring at the sullen sky.

"Mary?" I said. "Are you coming in?"

She glanced at me. Then she whispered, "Dad?" as though the news were dreadful. "It's going to snow."

It looked very likely to snow. The air was still, the whole world bleak and waiting. I could have agreed with her.

"Dad?" she repeated more urgently, probing me with large eyes—but what was I supposed to do? "It's going to snow!" she said.

"Come in, Mary. We don't have time to talk. Come in."

She entered the church ahead of me and climbed the steps in the narthex, then she started up the aisle toward the casket. She was seven years old. She was determined. Though robed and ready to preach, and though people sat face-forward on either side, I followed her.

Mary hesitated as she neared the chancel—but then took a final step and stopped.

She looked down into the casket. "Oh, no," she murmured, and I looked to see what she was seeing.

Odessa's eyes seemed closed with glue, her lips too pale, her color another shade than her own, a false, woody color.

Her skin seemed pressed into its patience. And the bridge of her nose suffered a set of glasses. Had Odessa worn glasses? Yes, sometimes. But these were perched on her face a little askew, so that one became aware of them for the first time. Someone else had put them there. What belonged to the lady any more, and what did not?

These were my speculations.

Mary had her own.

The child was reaching her hand toward the tips of Odessa's fingers, fingers like sticks of chalk; but she paused and didn't touch them. Suddenly she bent down and pressed her cheek to the fingers, then pulled back and stood erect.

"Dad!" she hissed. Mary turned and looked at me and did not blink but began to cry. "Dad!" she whispered, accusing, "It's going to snow, and Miz Williams is so cold." Immediately the tears were streaming down her face. "Dad!" she wept. "They can't put Miz Williams in the grave today. It's going to snow on her grave. It's going to snow on Miz Williams—"

All at once Mary stepped forward and buried her face in my robes. I felt the pressure of her forehead against my chest— and I was her father again, no pastor, and my own throat grew thick.

"Dad," sobbed Mary. "Dad, Dad, it's Christmas *Eve!*"

These were the tears. These were the tears my daughter cried at Christmas. What do I say to these tears? It is death my Mary met. It's the end of things. It's the knowledge that things *have* an end, good things, kind and blessed things, things new and rare and precious, and their goodness doesn't save them; that love has an end; that people have an end; that Odessa Williams, that fierce old lady who seized the heart of my Mary and possessed it just four days ago, who was so real in dim light, waving her arms to the music of the children, that *she* has an end, has ended, is gone, is dead.

How do I comfort these tears? What do I say?

I said nothing.

I knelt down. I took my Mary's face between my hands but

couldn't hold her gaze. I gathered her to myself and hugged her tightly, hugged her hard, hugged her until the sobbing passed from her body; and then I released her.

I watched her go back down the aisle like a poker soldier. She turned in a pew and sat with her mother. I saw that her lips were pinched into a terrible knot. No crying anymore. No questions anymore. Why should she ask questions when there were no answers given?

So: the funeral. And so: the sermon. And so I was the pastor again.

This was the text: "But there will be no gloom for her that was in anguish." The prophet Isaiah. It had seemed a perfect text, both for the season and for Odessa. "The people who walked in darkness have seen a great light," I read. That prophecy had come true in Jesus. It would become a truth again for the fierce old woman whose memorial this was. And for us too, since we were mourning now, but we would be celebrating tonight. I read: "For unto us a child is born, unto us a son is given—" *Christmas!* I said somewhere in my sermon. *Light is shining everywhere across the world, as light is shining first and perfectly in heaven! None who die in the Lord do die in darkness—*

But what were Isaiah and prophecy and all the sustaining truths of Christendom to my daughter Mary? She sat through the sermon with pinched lips and a sidelong stare. What was heaven to her? Nothing. Odessa had been something to her. You could touch and love Odessa. But Odessa was dead. The casket was closed. Death was something to her now, and maybe the only thing.

Later, at Oak Hill Cemetery, the people stood in great coats round the casket, shivering. My breath made ghosts in the air as I read of dust and ashes returning to dust and ashes. Mary said not a word nor held her mother's hand nor looked at me—except once.

When we turned from the grave she hissed, "Dad!" Her blue eyes flashing, she pointed at the ground. Then she pointed at the sky. At the roots of the grasses was a fine, white powder; in heaven was a darker powder coming down. It was snowing.

3.

We have several customs—in our church and in my family—on Christmas Eve: as to the church, we celebrate the evening always with a children's pageant of the birth of Jesus. There never was the pageant in which my children didn't participate. As for my family, we always open our Christmas presents after the pageant is over, when the glow is still upon us, when Thanne and I can watch the children and enjoy their joy. Nothing is dearer to me than the purity of their gladness then, the undiscordant music of their laughter then.

And nothing could grieve me more, than that one of my children should be sad and lose the blessings of these customs.

Therefore, I worried terribly for Mary all Thursday through. As it happened, she was to be *the* Mary of the pageant, the Virgin, the mother of the infant Jesus. At three in the afternoon I left church and went home to talk with her.

I found her alone in her bedroom, lying on the bed and gazing out the window, her chin on her wrists. Snow clouds caused a darkness within, but she'd left the lights off where she was.

I stood beside the bed and touched her. The pragmatic pastor was concerned whether this child could accomplish so public a role in so private a mood. The father simply wished he knew what his daughter was thinking.

"Mary," I said, "do you want us to get another Mary?"

She kept watching the snow come down. Slowly she shook her head. "No," she said. "I'm Mary."

I didn't think she'd understood me—and if she didn't, then my question must have sounded monstrous to her ears. "For the pageant, I mean," I said, "tonight."

But she repeated without the slightest variation, "I'm Mary."

Mary, Mary, so much Mary—but I wish you weren't sad. I wish I had a word for you. Forgive me. It isn't a kind world after all.

"You are Mary," I said. "I'll be with you tonight. It'll be all right."

We drove to church. The snow lay a loose inch on the ground. It swirled in snow-devils at the backs of the cars ahead of us. It held the grey light of the city near the earth, though this was now the night, and heaven was oblique in darkness. Surely, the snow covered Odessa's grave as well, a silent, seamless sheet.

These, I suppose, were Mary's thoughts, that the snow was cold on a new-dug grave. But Mary's thoughts confused with mine.

The rooms of the church were filled with light and noise, transfigured utterly from the low, funereal whispers of the morning. Black folk laughed. Parents stood in knots of conversation. Children darted, making ready for their glad performance, each in a different stage of dress, some in blue jeans, some in the robes of the shepherds two millennia and twenty lands away. Children were breathless and punchy. But Mary and I moved like spirits through this company, unnoticed and unnoticing. I was filled with her sorrow, while she seemed simply empty.

In time the wildness subsided. The actors huddled in their proper places. I sat with the congregation, two-thirds back on the right hand side. The lights in the sanctuary dimmed to darkness. The chancel glowed a yellow illumination. The pageant began, and soon my daughter stood with pinched lips, central to it all.

"My soul," said Mary, both Marys before a little Elizabeth— but she spoke so softly that few could hear, and my own soul suffered for her—"My soul," she murmured, "magnifies the Lord, and my spirit rejoices in God my Savior—"

And so: the child was surviving. But she was not rejoicing.

Some angels came and giggled and sang and left.

A decree went out.

Another song was sung.

And then three figures moved into the floodlit chancel: Joseph and Mary—and one other child, a sort of innkeeper-stage-manager who carried the manger, a wooden trough filled with old straw and a floppy doll in diapers.

The pageant proceeded, but I lost the greater part of it in watching my daughter.

For Mary stuck out her bottom lip and began to frown on the manger in front of her—to frown fiercely, not at all like the devout and beaming parent she was supposed to portray. At the *manger* she was staring, which stood precisely where Odessa's casket had sat that morning. She frowned so hard, blacking her eyes in such deep shadow, that I thought she would break into tears again, and my mind raced over things to do when she couldn't control herself any longer.

But Mary did not cry.

Instead, while shepherds watched over their flocks by night, my Mary played a part that no one had written into the script. Slowly she slipped her hand into the manger and touched the doll in diapers. She lifted its arm on the tip of her pointed finger, then let it drop. *What are you thinking, Mary?* All at once, as though she'd made a sudden decision, she yanked the doll out by its toes, and stood up, and clumped down the chancel steps, the doll like a dishrag at her side. People made mild, maternal sounds in their throats. The rhythm of a certain angel faltered. *Mary, where are you going? What are you doing?* I folded my hands at my chin and yearned to hold her, hide her, protect her from anything, from folly and from sorrow. But she carried the doll to the darkened sacristy on the right and disappeared through its door. *Mary? Mary!*

In a moment the child emerged carrying nothing at all.

Briskly she returned to the manger, up three steps as light as air, and down she knelt, and she gazed upon the empty straw with her palms together like the first Mary after all, full of adoration. And her face—Mary, my Mary, your face was radiant then!

O Mary, how I love you!

Not suddenly, but with a rambling, stumbling charge, there was in the chancel a multitude of the proudest heavenly host, praising God and shouting, "Glory to God in the highest!" But Mary knelt unmoved among them, and her seven-year face was smiling, and there was the flash of tears upon her cheeks, but they were not unhappy, and the manger, open, empty, seemed the receiver of them.

"Silent night, holy night—" All of the children were singing. "All is calm, all is bright—" The deeper truck-rumble of older voices joined them. "Round yon virgin mother and child—" The whole congregation was singing. Candlelight was passing hand to hand. A living glow spread everywhere throughout the church. And then the shock of recognition, and the soft flight followed: Dee Dee Lawrence allowed her descant voice its high, celestial freedom, and she flew. "Holy infant, so tender and mild—" *Mary, what do you see? What do you know that your father could not tell you? Mary, mother of the infant Jesus, teach me too.*

"Sleep in heavenly peace—" Having touched the crystal heaven Dee Dee descended. The congregation sighed. Everybody sang: "Sleep in heavenly peace."

Mary sat immediately beside me in the car as we drove home. A sifting snow made cones below the streetlights. It blew lightly across the windshield and closed us in a cotton privacy. I had been driving in silence.

Mary said, "Dad?"

I said, "What?"

She said, "Dad, Jesus wasn't in the manger. That wasn't Jesus. That was a doll." Ah, Mary, so you have the eyes of a realist now? And there is no pretending any more? It was a doll indeed. So death reveals realities—

"Dad?"

"What?"

She said, "Jesus, he doesn't *have* to be in the manger, does he? He goes back and forth, doesn't he? I mean, he came from heaven, and he was borned right here, but then he went back to heaven again, and because he came and went he's coming and going *all* the time—right?

"Right," I whispered. Teach me, child. It is so good to hear you talk again.

"The manger is empty," Mary said. And then she said more gravely, "Dad, Miz Williams' box is empty too. I figured it out. We don't have to worry about the snow." She stared out the windshield a moment, then whispered the next thing as softly as if she were peeping at presents: "It's only a doll in her box. It's like a big doll, Dad, and we put it away today. I figured it out. If Jesus can cross, if Jesus can go across, then Miz Williams, she crossed the same way too, with Jesus—"

Jesus, he don't never let one of us go. Never.

"Dad?" said Mary, who could ponder so much in her heart. "Why are you crying?"

Babies, babies, we be in the hand of Jesus, old ones, young ones, us and you together. Jesus, he hold us in his hand, and ain' no one goin' to snatch us out. Jesus, he don't never let one of us go. Never. Not ever—

"Because I have nothing else to say," I said to her. "I haven't had the words for some time now."

"Dad?"

"What?"

"Don't cry. I can talk for both of us."

It always was; it always will be; it was in the fullness of time when the Christ child first was born; it was in 1981 when my daughter taught me the times and the crossing of times on Christmas Eve; it is in every celebration of Christ's own crossing; and it shall be forever—that this is the power of a wise love wisely expressed: to transfigure the heart, suddenly, forever.

2. The Hornbill

In the rain forests of Africa there lives a common, awkward, ugly bird. But I will honor her as exquisite, because she is the cursive script of the Creator. When she flies, her flight is the handwriting of God. When she nests, God is imparting parables.

This bird inhabits the cathedral dark beneath high canopies of leaves. The vaulted space is green. Her world is loud with the shrieks of animals and dangerous with predators: jackals on the ground, the egg-eating bush-babies in the branches, monkeys and serpents and, wheeling over all, the eagle. Carnivores. She lives in a perilous place. But she lives. She flies. Swift on her wing, she eludes her enemies and feeds on the fruit of the climbing vines, the high and flowering trees. She flies. At all times it is her nature and her freedom to fly—except when she mothers her children.

She's called the hornbill because she's got a beak as big as a hollow log, and on top of that beak, a horn. Megaphone beak. Her cries would echo just because of that beak. It covers the whole of her face, and it sticks out in front of her like a spade—two spades clapped together, a cannon, a crag, a peninsula. This isn't a pretty bird. And affixed to the crest of her beak is a gross lump, a sort of a helmet, a casque, a gratuitous horn. The rhinoceros has a reason for his horn. Who knows why the hornbill carries hers?

The hornbill is a large and ugly bird.

No! But the hornbill is beautiful.

Watch her. Watch what she does. Watch what she does to *herself* for the sake of others.

When the time draws nigh that she should lay and love a clutch of eggs, this ugly bird transfigures herself by sweet degrees and sacrifice. She soars through the forest in search

of the perfect tree, which has a hollow trunk to receive herself
and her beak and her children. When she has found it, she
enters, and then she flies no more.

Immediately, with the help of her mate from the outside,
she sets to work to wall the doorway shut. Mud and dung make
a hard cement, a little interior fortress: no predator will break
in to terrorize her children or to eat them, no! They are
protected by her love. Out of her bowels comes their wall
against a treacherous world. She is their refuge while they are
tiny. *She* is their space a while.

But the wall that protects her children has imprisoned her.
There is no help for it. For the sake of her children she has
exchanged the spacious air of the forest for a tight, dark cell
and inactivity.

And what does this mean? It means that a mother has sacrificed her freedom, which is to fly.

But what does that mean? It means that she has sacrificed
her independence too. She is reduced to trusting absolutely
in her mate. Look: there is a slot in the wall she's constructed,
a vertical gap exactly the size of her beak. If the hornbill is to
survive in her cell, she has to eat. If she's going to eat, her
mate must bring her food—and then she will feed with pecu-
liar intimacy beak to beak through this slot, almost as though
she were a child herself: there was no kissing like this when she
was free. If her mate forsakes her, she will die. But for the love
of her children, a mother has chosen dependency.

Watch her. Watch that slot in the wall of dung. Food goes
in, but things come flying out of it. The hornbill is fastidious.
She twists around, and aims, and shoots her waste to the
outside world with a stinging accuracy. In this way she keeps
the nest immaculate. She can also burn the eye of a bush-baby
peeping in. She can change the mind of a monkey who
thought to snatch a meal.

But soon, when her children are hatched and very tender,
something else comes flying out of the slot, something so

terribly beautiful that every parent must gasp with understanding, and every Christian stand in awe.

Watch: it is feathers. One by one the hornbill's feathers sail into the air and flutter down to earth. But these are not the down of her breast; they are the longest, strongest feathers of her wing. And this is an immediate act of mercy for her children, because the shafts of these feathers could wound them as she moves about in the tiny space. Therefore, she plucks her primary feathers with a monstrous beak.

And what does that mean? It means that this mother has torn flight from herself. It means that she has sacrificed her very nature for the sake and the saving of her children.

Therefore the hornbill is passing beautiful!

She is the very parable of love.

All these things spake Jesus unto the multitude in parables; and without a parable spake he not unto them: that it might be fulfilled which was spoken by the prophet, saying, I will open my mouth in parables; I will utter things which have been kept secret from the foundation of the world.

Who is the hornbill? Whom does she signify?

Read her, as once the ancient Christians read the whole book of nature—the mind of God made visible. And then tell me, Christian: who is she?

Who chose to leave the infinite sphere of heaven—willingly, willingly, compelled by his loving alone? Who denied himself celestial flight for the sake of a people and walled himself inside this world, in time and space and flesh, that he might be the refuge of the weary?

Who diminished himself to dependency—a perfect, prayerful, infant dependency upon another—for the sake of a people who had thought themselves so independent?

Who plucked himself of power? Who sheared himself of his deific might and radiant glory lest it harm us when we came near to him? Who emptied himself and became a baby, swaddled in humility, cradled in wood, flightless, bound to die?

Who loved us that much? Who loved us so purely? Who loved us by such sweet degrees of sacrifice? Of course! We are reading Christmas in an awkward bird.

O Jesus, born in our darker, smaller world! Christ, come down to nourish and usher us into thy brighter, spacious heavens! O my Savior, gentle in flesh beside me here—thou art the hornbill! Thou art not ugly. Cumbered, maybe, to be here. Not ugly at all, but beautiful.

I love thee, Jesus. I love thee with all my heart.

3. A Psalm at the Sunrise

Omnipotens sempiterne Deus!
Almighty God, the Everlasting, Thou! I cannot look stead-
fastly at the sun and not go blind. Holiness exceeds my sight—
though I know it is, as I know thou art.

Aeterne Deus omnium rerum Creator!
Thou art above all created things. To everything made, thou
art the Other. Greater than thee there is no world; in thee all
worlds have being; and I take my trivial, mortal way upon the
smallest sphere of all. How shall I hope to see thee and not
die?

Lux Mundi!
But in thy mercy thou shinest down upon the things that thou
hast made. They brighten in thy light. Every morning they
reflect thee. I wake to an effulgence of mirrors, and lo: I see.

Misericors Deus!
For my sake, for my poor fleshly sight, thou changest thy
terrible holiness here before me into glory—the visible light,
the doxology I can see. I rise and look around, and I cry praise
to thee.

Deus, incommutabilis virtus, lumen aeternum!
From thee to me it is a mighty diminution: ever the same, thou
makest thy presence manifest in things that are both mutable
and common. But from me to thee it is epiphany: gazing at
things most common, suddenly I see thy light, thy glory, and
thy face.

Nobiscum Deus!
Then what shall I say to thee but *Deo Gratias?* Thanks be to
God.

Deo gratias!
For the dew that damps the morning grasses is a baptism, always, always renewing the earth. And the air remembers that once it ushered down the dove that was the breath of God. And I myself inhale the rinsed spirit of the morning air and am renewed.

Deo gratias!
For dawn, in the chalices of the clouds, brims them with a bloody wine, a running crimson. And this is a sign to me. The sun is coming.

Deo gratias!
For the sun, when it breaks at the horizon, transfigures everything. And this is a gift to me. For the transfiguration itself persuades my soul of sunrise.

Jesui filii Dei, gratias!
For I have seen a baby sleeping in a shaft of sunlight, and behold: in the curve of every eyelash was a small sun cupped. From these fringes, tiny rays shot forth to sting me. Sunrise at the far horizon was sunrise near me in this infant.

Et verbum caro factum est—
For the baby suddenly opened her mouth and yawned. And into that pink cavern rushed the sunlight, trembling and flashing like a living thing. But it was thee, bright God, in the mouth of a mortal infant.

"Ecce ego vobiscum sum—"
For the baby woke to the morning and saw me close beside her, and she smiled. Ah, God! What an epiphany of smiling that was! My own transfiguration! For this was the primal light, the glory of the morning, thy splendor and thy face before me come.

Deo gratias, cuius gloria!
Then glory be to thee, Father, Son, and Holy Spirit, as it was in the beginning, is now, and ever shall be, *saecula saeculorum.*

Amen.

4. The Christmas Story

Once upon a time—

Tell this story in a generous voice. Hush your voices, men, when you enter its passages; and women, almost whisper. When you speak of loving, seem to love. Describing sorrow, be sad. Let fear come through a harried voice, and gladness come with laughter, and triumph sound like exultation.

Half of the life of the story is the story's teller. Your voice and face and body give it form. It is you whom the children hear and see. They will not distinguish. It is you who will love or not, and so the story will or will not love.

Touch the child, sir, when you tell it. Ma'am, tell it to children. If you do not tell it at all, it isn't. It doesn't exist for them. Then tell it. Do not neglect it, but tell it.

Once upon a time the world was dark, and the land where the people lived was deep in darkness. It was as dark as the night in the daytime. It had been dark for so long that the people had forgotten what the light was like. This is what they did: they lit small candles for themselves and pretended it was day. But the world was a gloomy place, and the people who walked in darkness were lonelier than they knew, and the lonely people were sadder than they could say.

But God was in love with the world.

God looked down from heaven and saw that the earth was stuck, like a clock, at midnight. "No," he said. "This isn't good. It's time to make time tick again. Time, time," said the mighty God, "to turn the earth from night to morning."

And God was in love with the people especially.

He saw their little candlelight, and he pitied their pretending. "They think they see," he said, "but all they see is

shadow, and people are frightened by shadows. Poor people!"
he said. "They wonder why they are afraid." God watched the
people move about like fireflies in the night, and he shook his
head. "Poor people, pretending to be happy," he said. "Well,
I want them to be happy. It's time," declared the Lord our
God. "It's time to do a new thing! I'll shatter their darkness.
I will send the sunlight down so they can see and know that
they are seeing!"

God so loved the world, that he sent his only son into the
world itself. And this is how he did it:

Once upon a time, when the whole earth was cloaked in a
cloud of darkness, God in heaven turned to his angel and said,
"Gabriel."

And the angel said, "What, Lord?"

And God said, "Go. Go down. Go tell my people remarkable news—"

*Parents, if you haven't already told your children the story, who has?
What sort of Gabriel brought it to them? Don't you know that the teller
shapes the tale?*

*Grandparents, are you satisfied to let mumbling Rumor garble this
marvelous story for your grandchildren? Should they piece it together
themselves, from Christmas carols and that dead set, that mercenary
invasion, that box of empty sentiment and silliness, the television? "The
true meaning of Christmas"—indeed!*

*No, but faith should tell the tale. And love should serve it to the
children lovingly. For it recounts no less than the beginning of the child's
salvation.*

*Then you should tell it to the little ones whom you love, whose spirits
you are responsible for. You tell it. You.*

*Fathers, make a holy time in which nothing distracts you and nothing
delights your children except this story. Mothers, prepare a holy space
in a corner of your home. Time and space will prove the story important.
Grandma, Grandpa, present a holy attitude. You reach to an ancient
bedrock for this story. Both the age in your face and the love in your*

eye will convince the child of that, and of its truth.

Then tell the story whole, beginning to end, all of a piece, and seamless.

Say, "Child, I want to tell you a story beautiful and true. It actually happened; it happened for you."

Say, "Once upon a time, the angel Gabriel was sent from God—"

So there was an angel flying through the night. So swiftly he flew that nobody noticed. Across the continents the angel went, to a particular province named Galilee, to a city named Nazareth, and then in that city to one particular house, to one particular woman sleeping in that house. Her name was Mary. She was young and blameless and lovely in her bed, as innocent as the lily. Her lashes were long and black. She was a virgin, but she dreamed of a man named Joseph, because they were betrothed and would marry in four months' time. She was smiling in her sleep.

The angel Gabriel appeared at Mary's bedside and began to grow bright.

Light beamed in her bedroom. So Mary frowned a little. She turned in her sleep and she sighed.

Brighter and brighter grew the angel, until he blazed like the sun.

God in heaven whispered, "Gabriel, why do you hesitate? Talk to her."

So the angel opened his mouth and spoke to the woman. "Hail," he said.

But the angel's voice was like thunder.

Poor Mary awoke with a terrible start. Her eyes flew open, and she saw the brilliant light beside her, and she heard the glorious greeting in her ears, and she caught her breath, did Mary, because she was afraid—

Do you see? Do you see? The reason why the story must be told by a human mouth to human ears with human faith and affection is that a story is always more than information that some poor kid must labor to understand. A story is a world, my dears, both radiant and real—a world into which the child is invited, and she enters.

And it is the telling of the tale that causes this world to be.

The telling encourages the child to believe its being.

The telling calls her into it so that she more than knows: she actually experiences.

In the instant that the child imagines the light that Mary sees, and cares for Mary, and fears with her—in that same instant your child has departed this veiled existence and entered the world where God is un-veiled, bright and present and active and loving. And which of these worlds is real? Why, both. But the latter gives meaning to the former. The latter is revelation.

The child must be enchanted.

And the story must continue to be told.

Continue, then, in a husky human voice—

When the angel said "Hail" in the middle of the night, like bright explosions in her bedroom, poor Mary jumped and covered her mouth and could not talk, because she was afraid.

God in heaven whispered, "Hurry, Gabriel. Comfort the woman."

So the angel said, "Hush, Mary." The angel softened his glorious voice and murmured like rain in the night, "Mary, hush. The dear God loves you, don't you know? God favors you, and the Lord is with you."

God favors me? Mary was trembling. Her mind was racing in the unnatural light. This greeting of the angel troubled her. *What does it mean? What is he saying?* she thought. *Why would an angel come to me?*

"Mary, do not be afraid," said the angel, still more gently— and the light grew warmer than bright, and it touched her, just on the forehead, with a single beam of kindness. So Mary grew calmer; her mind grew quiet; and she began to listen.

"Behold," said the angel, "you will conceive in your womb and bring forth a son, and you shall call his name Jesus."

A baby? thought Mary. *A baby?*

"Quickly, Gabriel," said God in heaven. "Tell her quickly what this means."

And quickly the angel did a comely thing: he stopped speaking, and he started to sing. So marvelous was the meaning of this baby, that it wanted a song for the telling.

"Mary," sang the angel:

Mary, the child of thy labor shall be great;
The Son of the Most High shall he be called;
And God shall give him the throne of his father David;
Over the house of Jacob shall he reign
Forever and ever: his kingdom shall have no end.

A baby? thought Mary in spite of the music. How dear was the promise. How deeply she longed for it. But there was a problem she couldn't ignore. Desire was troubled by that problem, and Mary astonished herself. She actually spoke to the angel.

"How can this be?" she blurted—and the angel stopped singing, and God in heaven began to smile.

Well, maybe the angel didn't understand the nature of human bodies. Some things had to happen first for other things to happen second. "How can this be?" said Mary meekly on her bed. "I'm not married, you see. I don't have a husband yet."

That was the problem. Not the greatness of the baby, not his kingship, nor that the kingdom would last forever—but that the baby needed, first, a father.

There came a strange sound in Mary's bedroom then, like the creaking of the walls, or the cracking of the universe. It was an angel chuckling. For the thing that he was telling Mary was a miracle, after all. The new thing God was doing didn't depend on nature. First things needn't come first anymore, and the baby would have a father, but not the kind that Mary imagined.

So the angel continued, in a happy melody, to sing:

Mary, the Holy Spirit shall come upon thee;
The power of God shall overshadow thee.
And what shall they call the child that is born of thee?
Why, they shall call him holy! The Son of God!

Mary said nothing for a moment. She was grinning and gazing at an angel, and her eyes were bright with the light. A baby, and more than a baby, oh! The Son of God. Then God would father this baby. Oh!

The angel stopped singing and murmured, "Mary?"

Mary raised her eyebrows and stretched her grin from ear to ear. "Mmm?"

"With God," the angel assured her, "nothing will be impossible."

So Mary, kneeling on her bed; Mary, bowing as lovely as the lily, whispered, "Behold—" Deep, deep inside her stomach she felt the giggles coming. "Behold," she said, "I am the handmaid of the Lord. Be it unto me according to your word—"

Which word was: Mary is going to have a baby! Yes!

So the angel was done, and he dimmed. The bright light faded from her bedroom. Gabriel vanished altogether. But Mary didn't mind the darkness now.

A baby!

Oh, she jumped from her bed, and the giggles tickled her throat. Oh, she clapped her hands and twirled about, and her dark hair flew like a glory around her head. Oh, the virgin was laughing now, for the virgin was going to have a baby!

So who had news for the telling now? And who would burst if she couldn't tell it? Mary!

So now there was a blameless, beautiful woman running through the world, the dark world, as fast as she could go. None of the people noticed her go. She didn't mind. She was grinning and full of good news. South she ran, to a particular province named Judea, to a particular hill, and on that hill to one particular house and one particular woman in that house, her friend, her cousin Elizabeth.

"Elizabeth, hello!"

Just as the angel had greeted Mary, Mary greeted Elizabeth, and Elizabeth began immediately to laugh.

And just as the angel had sung his celestial song for her, she sang a song for Elizabeth.

"My soul," sang Mary, "O cousin, my soul doth magnify the Lord. My spirit rejoiceth in God my Savior. He is keeping his promises to us. Elizabeth! I'm going to have a baby!"

So then—in the middle of the gloomy world there were two women laughing. They laughed till they couldn't laugh any more, and then they began to weep for gladness.

And God looked down from heaven and saw them. And the Lord God smiled.

This, good parents, is the reason why you are telling your child the story, why you are weaving its marvelous world around her: because of love.

Because you love her. Surely that. I scarcely need to mention that.

But also because you love the Lord whose birth you are retelling, and this is the finest way to express your love and to celebrate his birthday both at once. That, too.

But more than that, because the Lord Jesus loves your child; and how shall she know it except she also feels it?

It isn't enough just to say it. That piece of knowledge fits like a stone in the pocket, but not in the heart. It is necessary that she should be loved, that she dwell within the light of that love, that love lift her up and take her to its breast, that she breathe love and laugh love and sleep in its sweet dominion—and so experience its security, its peace, and so believe in love.

This is not a matter of the intellect, that she should think about it. This is a matter of the heart. It isn't explained. It happens.

This is not a lesson to be learned. This is an event. And Jesus, whose story this is, encounters your child when she enters his story. And Jesus says to the child, "Hail." And what then? Why, then your child begins to grin. And her eyes grow bright with the light of the Lord. The darkness of this world is shattered for her. The sunlight shines. For she has heard her Jesus speak, and she has been transfigured by his love. She is God's own beloved.

But you, good parents and goodly grandparents—this is also the reason why you must tell the tale unto your children.

For between you and the child there is already a weaving of human love, and the threads of that earthly weave become the holier threads of Jesus' story and his love. The shape of your love shall pattern the truer love of God when it comes—as when an artist models in clay what he shall finish in bronze or in gold.

For between you and the child already is trust, and sympathy, and a common memory, and mercy and discipline together, and triumphs, and failures, and anger, and forgiveness. These are the threads of an active love. But when it is you who tell the story in your own voice unto your own child, these also become the delicate threads that define and shape the story, in her mind first, and then in her heart. They weave Jesus. Better yet, Jesus rides the weave; so human experience is elevated to heavenly experience. In the story, all of these become the relationship between the child and God: trust and sympathy—and love. Slowly, then, but rightly and wondrously, God takes your place in the heart of the child. God becomes the truer, holier, brighter parent.

You tell the story to your child, then, in order to deliver your child to God, that God should adopt her and keep her forever and forever safe.

Because you love her, you see.

But the baby isn't born yet. Talk on, dear parents. Sing on, sweet Gabriels, till the whole of the song is sung.

When Mary had returned to Nazareth, the man whom she was going to marry began to notice changes in her.

Now the world was very dark in those days. And people are scared in the dark, you know. But they are specially scared of changes in the dark—like moving the furniture, or changing your habits, or changing your mind; because if people don't understand these changes, they bump against them and hurt themselves and cry. In the long, long night, when people had only their candles for seeing, change was considered a dangerous thing.

Therefore, Joseph became suspicious of the changes that he saw in Mary.

"Why do you smile all the time?" he said.

And she said, "Oh, you'll see."

"Why are you always giggling? Why do you laugh all the time? And what is that strange light in your eyes?" said Joseph.

And Mary said, "You'll see."

Well, soon Joseph saw, and what he saw distressed him.

He saw that her tummy was growing big. Joseph saw that Mary was going to have a baby, and this upset him, because he wasn't the baby's father. But he truly loved Mary, so he felt hurt as well as sad, because somebody else must be the baby's father.

"How did this happen?" he asked her.

But she said, "It was the Holy Spirit," and poor Joseph grew simply miserable.

"Mary is lying to me," he said.

In those days the dark world had some dark rules by which a man could put a woman away—and then it would be as if they had never been married at all. If a woman had a baby by someone besides her husband, then her husband could put the woman away. That was the rule.

One night Joseph lay in bed and thought about this rule.

He said the words out loud. He said, "I will put her away," and he almost started to cry.

He was a good man, was Joseph. He didn't want his Mary to suffer the shame of the gossip of the people who walked in darkness. "O wagging tongues!" he shouted. "O wagging, nasty tongues, you shall not hurt my Mary!" Therefore, he decided to put her away privately, so that no one would know what he was doing, or the sinful thing that she had done—to be with child before they married.

With such heavy thoughts on his mind, poor Joseph fell asleep.

Then God in heaven turned to his angel.

"Gabriel," said God.

And the angel said, "What, Lord?"

"Go down," said God. "Go down right now. Tell Joseph the truth. The man is blinded by the darkness. He thinks that Mary has committed a sin. Go! Go!"

So a light grew bright in Joseph's sleep, and the brightness was a dream, but the light was the angel Gabriel, so close to the man that he shined inside his mind.

"Joseph, son of David," said the angel.

Joseph slept on; but Joseph heard and saw, and he remembered. And the more he heard, the happier he became, until there was a man in Nazareth who was smiling in his sleep.

"Joseph, do not be afraid to take Mary for your wife," said the angel. "The baby conceived in her is of the Holy Spirit. Mary didn't sin. Mary doesn't lie. Mary is going to have a baby boy, and you shall call him Jesus, and this is what his name means: that he will save his people from their sins."

Listen, listen! Sin is the darkness of the world! This baby shall be its light, for he shall shine in the dark and take its sin away. *Emmanuel* is the infant that shall be born, which means: *God with us.*

Joseph, God is keeping his promises. Joseph, something wonderful is happening—

Even in his sleep the man was smiling as broad as a barn. When he woke, he was positively grinning. The people in Nazareth noticed the change in him, and they became suspicious.

"Why do you smile all the time?" they asked. "Why are you always giggling?"

"Oh," said Joseph, "I'm getting married."

But even after they were married Mary and Joseph seemed odd to the people in darkness.

"Why are you laughing all the time?" they demanded. "Why don't you fuss or fight? And what is that strange light in your eyes?"

"You'll see," they said. They giggled and said, "You'll see."

So Mary grew big and bigger with her child.

And Joseph put his hand on her tummy and laughed because he felt the baby kick.

And God looked down from heaven too. And the Lord God smiled.

For this is what the story says: that the Lord made a baby ball of himself and dropped into our hard, material world. God with us.

But that is also what the story does: makes a palpable person of the high transcendent Deity, a living and intimate being who strides into the child's world to love her where she is, just as she had crept into his story to meet him where he was, in infancy incarnate.

The Lord and the story, they establish relationship.

But relationship, dear parents and wiser grandparents (wonder at this thing: it is a marvel of continuing creation)—relationship creates and confers identity.

From the beginning the child received her identity in relationship to you; thereby came her name, and with her name her shape, her image, her very character. The name you gave her consciously, perhaps. Shape and image and character she received as an unconscious birthright: you gave them to her because you bore her. You gave them to her in the natural process of raising her. But name and shape and image and character, first being yours, became hers—became her—in relationship to you.

Likewise this marvelous, seminal, progenitive story. In the hearing of it, the child comes to know her Lord and his love. But in that relationship she also comes to know herself. Who is born in the story? Why, Jesus. But who is born in the telling of the story? Why, your child is—reborn. For here she receives and is persuaded of a name: Beloved of God. And herein the children of God are shaped, and character is accorded them, a way to be and to behave; and the presence of God (the actual presence of God!) empowers that character, that the children might truly love as God loves them. And since it is God both shaping and empowering them, what then? Then theirs is the image of God again. The image broken in sin is renewed in the faces of the children.

Ah, parents, how could you not sit down and tell your children such a story? However could you justify neglecting it? For this is the Gospel itself—which, if they do not hear it, how can they believe? And telling it is nothing less than proclamation.

So tell it, tell it, with calm simplicity and a cosmic serenity. With faith. And thou dost name thy children in the telling, as thou thyself wast named.

Tell it with a generous voice, especially this passage to come, as familiar to thee as the rising of the sun.

And hush thy voice, O man, when that thou enterest this passage. And woman, almost whisper.

For this is the fullness of time, the fullness of heavenly love for us: the birth.

Now it came to pass in those dark days, that there went out a command from Caesar that all of the people should be counted. "A census," he decreed. "Citizens, go to the cities of your ancestors, to be counted according to families there."

So people began to travel.

So Joseph, too, obeyed the command. He and Mary traveled south together, to the province named Judea, to a particular city of David called Bethlehem, but in that city to no particular house at all, for they had no house in Bethlehem. Joseph was a descendant of David; that's why he came to Bethlehem. But there were hundreds and hundreds of others descended from David; the city was crowded with people, and that's why there were no houses nor rooms at all where Joseph could lay his Mary down to rest for a while and stay.

Even the inn was full.

But the night was dark and cold. The night was deep and lonely.

And Mary was huge with her child and tired.

She wasn't grinning any more, was Mary. She was groaning. "Joseph," she whispered, "it's time. Oh, Joseph," she said, "the baby is coming. It's time."

"Mary, can you wait a little longer?"

"No," she said.

"Mary, there's no place for us."

"It's time," she said.

So Joseph went running through the streets of the city. People were sleeping. Nobody noticed. Nobody answered his knocking.

So this is all he could find: a stable where travelers tethered their beasts when they slept. A little shelter against the night.

"Mary," he said when he led her there, "do you mind?"

"No," she said.

"Can you lie on the straw?"

"It's time," she said and knelt down.

So there it was that she brought forth her firstborn son; and she wrapped him in swaddling clothes and laid him in a manger, because there was no room for them in the inn.

In the beginning, before there was a world at all, God spoke. And this is the first thing ever the Lord God said. God said: "Let there be light." And there was light.

Light is the first thing God created. And this, and all things, he made with his creating Word; for he said it, and it was.

In the beginning, then, was the Word, and the Word was with God, and the Word was God—for what was God unto the world, except that he spoke? Or where would the world be if God had never spoken?

The Word was in the beginning with God. All things were made through him, and without him was not anything made that was made.

In him was life, and the life was the light of every people.

*The light shines in the darkness, and the darkness has not over-
come it.*

*Nevertheless, there came an aeon, once upon a time in human history,
when the world was dark, and the land where the people lived was deep
in darkness, and the light of God was hidden. It was dark as the night
in the daytime. It had been dark so long that the people had forgotten
what the light was like.*

But God was in love with the people.

*Therefore, God spoke again, the second time. But the Lord God said
what he had said in the beginning, before there was a world at all. He
said, "Let there be light!"*

*And so the Word came down into the world that the Word himself
had made.*

*For the Word became flesh and dwelt among us, full of grace and
truth; we have beheld his glory, glory as of the only Son from the Father.*

*This, dear parents, grandparents, is all that we have said: that every
time you tell the story, the first light shines again. Your words give
opportunity to the Word, that the children might behold him. For to all
who receive him, who believe in his name, he gives power to become
children of God.*

This is what we've said. No more than this.

And so you shall, in faith, continue your own saying, even to the end.

And there were shepherds in that same dark country, abid-
ing in the fields, keeping watch over their flocks by night.

And God turned to his angel. And God said, "Gabriel."

And the angel answered, "Yes, Lord?"

And the Lord God said, "Go down. All of the people must
know what I am doing. Tired and lonely and scattered and
scared, all of the people must hear it. Go, good Gabriel. Go
down again. Go tell a few to tell the others, till every child has
heard it. Go!"

And so it was that an angel of the Lord appeared to the
weary shepherds. Their dark was shattered, for the glory of

the Lord shone round about them, and they were sore afraid.

The angel said to them, "Don't be afraid."

But the light was like a hard and holy wind, and the shepherds shielded their faces with their arms.

"Hush," said the angel, "hush," like the west wind. "Shepherds, I bring you good news of great joy, and not only for you but for all of the people. Listen."

So shepherds were squinting and blinking, and shepherds began to listen, but none of them had the courage to talk or to answer a thing.

"For unto you is born this day in the city of David," said the angel, "a Savior, who is Christ the Lord. And this will be a sign for you: you will find the babe wrapped in swaddling clothes and lying in a manger."

Suddenly the sky itself split open, and like the fall of a thousand stars, the light poured down. There came with the angel a multitude of the heavenly host, praising God and saying:

> Glory to God in the highest,
> And on earth, peace—
> Peace to the people with whom he is pleased!

But hush, you shepherds. Hush in your wonder. For the choral singing soon was ended. The hosts ascended, and the sky was closed again. And then there came a breeze and a marvelous quiet and the simple dark of the night. It was just that, no terror in that then. It was only the night, no deeper gloom than evening. For not all of the light had gone back into heaven. The Light of the World himself stayed down on earth and near you now.

And you can talk now. Try your voices. Try to speak. Ah, God has given you generous voices, shepherds. Speak.

So then, this is what the shepherds said to one another:

"Let us," they said, "go over to Bethlehem and see this thing that has happened, which the Lord has made known to us."

So the shepherds got up and ran as fast as they could to the city of Bethlehem, to a particular stable in that city, and in that stable they gazed on one particular baby, lying in a manger.

Then, in that moment, everything was fixed in a lambent, memorial light.

For there was the infant, just waking, just lifting his arms to the air and making sucking motions with his mouth. The holy child was hungry. And there was his mother, lying on straw as lovely as the lily and listening to the noises of her child. "Joseph?" she murmured. And there was Joseph, as sturdy as a barn, just bending toward his Mary. "What?" he whispered.

And the shepherds' eyes were shining for what they saw.

Exactly as though it were morning and not the night, the shepherds went out into the city and began immediately to tell everyone what the angel had said about this child. They left a trail of startled people behind them, as on they went, both glorifying and praising God.

But Mary did not so much as rise that night. She received the baby from Joseph's hands, then placed him down at her breast while she lay on her side on straw. With one arm she cradled the infant against her body. On the other arm, bent at the elbow, she rested her head; and she gazed at her small son sucking. Mary lowered her long, black lashes and watched him and loved him and murmured, "Jesus, Jesus," for the baby's name was Jesus.

"Joseph?" she said without glancing up.

And Joseph said, "What?"

But Mary fell silent and said no more. She was keeping all these things—all that had happened between the darkness and the light—and pondering them in her heart.

5. The Christ Mass
(Back Through Headlong Time)

I (Strophe)

How did they kill the coyote?
They hardly knew.

They chased him, they raced him in exhaustless
Belly-treaded snowmobiles,
Snaring space on the open fields,
Stitching his tracks, exhausting him.

Wind in their beards, laughter cracking their teeth,
The sun a silver bugling on the snows,
They sliced the sound, they rode the brightness
Like tears on mirrors, exhausting him.

He squirt forward between their flanking,
Snapped tail to corner from a looping pincer,
Squeezed speed from his ribs—ran, ran,
His tongue blown backward at the ear.

How did they kill the coyote?
They never knew

That when they rode their mechanical rattlers
To the horizon, the coyote crack-plunged
Through the nooning crust
Of old spring snow—five feet in a white pit.

Exhausted, he could not leap nor dig long
Nor wait a better day or nourishment,
But lay down in a lather, dying,
Till the foam was frozen on his shoulder.

How did they kill the coyote?
Like a roach in a teacup.

(ANTISTROPHE)

Jesus was born with hair
  With needle teeth
  A milk-blue breath
Four paws walking and aware:
A natal song we sing for thee;
In terra canunt angeli.

Mary his mother licked
  All lovingly
  His rheumy eye
With a doting tongue and quick:
And lullabies we croon to thee;
In terra canunt angeli.

Flesh of the flesh of beasts
  Creation's ward
  Who was its Lord
Born to host, to meat our feasts:
Astonished hymns and litanies
In terra canunt angeli.

Cub of Creation, go
  Break from thy den
  Run among men
Cross our Colorado snows—
And prove what sort of beasts we be.
In terra canunt angeli,
Et lamentantur archangeli.

II (Strophe)

And the wolf—
How did they kill the wolf?
Wrap tallow-fat
Around a knife
Set upright: Freeze
Fat and blade in
A block of ice
Point prominent.

But the wolf—
How did they kill the wolf?
He ran his tongue
Like a muslin
Of flesh across
The fat: drool from
Joints in his jaw
Numbed the tongue-cuts.

How did they kill the wolf?
His drooling dropped
Blood: blood he lapped
Blood he hungered
Lord so fiercely
His stomach seized
At warm rich blood.

The wolf? The wolf—
Bled forth his food
Swallowed gulped and
Did not know he
Was his prey: he
Praised God that all
He wished he had.

Oh you blesséd
Block of Sweetblood!—
The wolf: he drained
And drank his life
By the self-same
Lacerated
Howling organ. . . .

Speak to me speak
To me speak to
Me how did they
Kill the wolf? *Did*
They kill the wolf?
Did he know he
Craved his own blood?

(ANTISTROPHE)

Mary delivered Jesus on her knees,
Pushed him head-downward to the scalloped earth
Bare between her knees, pressed for all her worth
With both hands folded on her belly, squeezed
Her lids and lips, her teeth, her being *(Please)*
To drive him down, to bring him to his birth;
Mary *(God! God! Father of this hard hurt,*
Please! Let your baby come!) begged on her knees—

And this is how God solved her maidenhood:
She tore.
In a rush the flesh burst like a breached door.
Blood poured
Before and with and on the infant. Blood:
His first milk, air, his swaddling—and all his mother's
    good.

III (STROPHE)

But even the cow was nursed at the birthing.
"Y'hear that woofing?" said Edward. "She's choked
At the wrong end. Wear my boots." And we went.

Since she'd been laboring, lowing all night long
To bring her calf breech-wise into the world,
Edward tied a cord around the hooves
That hung beneath her tail like tails,
And tugged. Her sides heaved. He put a raw boot
To her hip to help himself and pulled
Till they sweat together, the calf between.
"Let go let go let go"—but who was holding?

The sun breached the horizon. Fog crawled the fields
Burning. Me. I took her blameless gaze.

As if suddenly convinced to risk it—"Wow!"
The calf plunged out and Edward sat backward
With a slick busybody bumping for footing
Now, *now* on his impossible pants.

But what I recall with a dazzled gratitude
Seeing, was the balloon of fluid that followed
This calf into the world, a globe no one had promised.
Morning sunlight fused within and set it glowing,
Till Edward took his thick farmer's finger
And stabbed the bladder, collapsing it—and
Its heavy water washed the earth. Amen.

(ANTISTROPHE)

There came a moment when
Resting on her pallet
    Mary sat upright
As though remembering
As though she'd murmur, "I know—
    I know it now."

But she held her peace, did Mary.
A smile like blotted water
    Darkened her mouth,
Like a new rain freshet
Spilled on the ledges below
    Her eyes: *I know*—

She tipped her head to the side
As though attending to
    A word at her vulva.
Does melting make a sound?
Her hair ran all on her left
    Breast down: *I know*—

Then she touched the man beside her
Lightly, to leave this moment
    Undisturbed,
And whispered like a spray
Of roses, roses: "Joseph,
    My water broke."

IV (Strophe)

Is it the menses that teaches a girl
To tread ground with a guardant step as though
Hobbled by dread or by great sympathy?
When does she learn the earth is her sister? . . .

Did you, the farmer peered, *swaller that 'seed?*
His grandchild paused, her face lost in a smile
Of watermelon rind, frowning because
She trusted his decrees as trust a priest.

Swaller a seed, he said, *your tummy swells
And soon you have a baby, Fi-fo-fum!*
Well, soon the child was running the back fields,
Troubled, beseeching God about a seed.

Illinois soil is black as blankets. She
Stopped at a corn crib. Grandpa, his hands tucked
Under the bib of his overalls, gross
Contentment, came, and gazed away from her.

Illinois evening skies are amethyst;
Corduroy cornfields rug the farther ground;
The nearer ground is irrigated with
A running darkness down the rows. Black blood.

You worried? Grandpa wondered of the west-
Northwest. His grandchild did not nod. She frowned.
'Cause eatin' seeds, he said, *it ain't no bane.
Earth ate a load of seed, and look at her.*

*Look at her swell—green and so pretty, girl,
I want to cry. She's pregnant, don't you know.
I hear the woman low, hear the dirt down
Low, like a mama moaning lullabies.*

Illinois cornfields form a church of pews;
Grandpa, slouching in the arched crib as priests
Slouch twice the Verba, had an acolyte
Beside him, lighting candles in her eyes.

All them seedlings are her litter, he said,
Her babies, curled and yearning to the birth.
Listen: hear the blood rush? Hear the deep
Roots drinking life? She heard. She heard. She learned—

That she stood on the holy woman, Earth,
Stood on a great womb fat to teeming young.
And when she walked it was with garden steps
She went—as women, crushing nothing, go.

Come fall, Fi-fo-fum, Grandpa winked, *come fall,*
He said, *we'll grind her corn to make our bread.*
—That night engendered in a girlchild love
And a deep dread, both, for Earth and for her
Self, forever.

(ANTISTROPHE)

Jesus was strong, strong as the storm;
He churned the waters ere he was born.

Jesus was merry, imp of the sun;
He caused the waters to giggle and run.

He raised a wave that slapped the shore
Not after birth—a month before!

O mother of our infant king,
How *did* he such a wondrous thing?

(And Mary remembers the primal days
With shining eyes and quiet praise)—

While I bathed naked in the lake
He kicked, for all creation's sake.

My belly punched a pretty wave:
'Twas him in a hurry, hasty and brave.

Oh, mine was a monstrous pod to bear,
Lord of the seas, the land and air:

But while he lingered in his daughter
I was the weather that dashed the water;

I was a planet, God's low girl,
A green, complete, and turning world.

    Earth! Sweet earth!
    With love we burst.

V (Strophe)

In the zygote seed
All we need.

Parts die:
Male and female
In travail;
Natures human and divine
Still perishing
Till IS is one one satisfies
And all is me
But none am I
Since AM is pure divinity.

The zygote cell:
Emmanuel,
Being indivisible.

Tell me why,
In the first spring rain,
Do they cry
And the fields hiss pain?
It's we, sweet Jesus, we—
The grain deceased in thee.

(ANTISTROPHE)

When Gabriel departed and all glory,
And water was boiling, and I remembered the coals
I'd blown before the angel stood before me;

When I knelt down with tongs to spread those coals
(My left hand on my thigh, my right hand reaching)
Scarcely recalling bright news for clay bowls;

When someone called my name in the street—each thing
Common in my lot, equable as sand—
Then, just then, I felt . . . I call it a "stitching"

In my right side, low down and deep. *Stand! Stand
Up, Mary,* I thought; but I could not move.
This ache in my pelvis, this light larval spasm—

I, who had never known motion in the caves of
My womanhood, cried: "The egg . . . drops! Oh, my love!"

Reprise

Christmas and his Incarnation
Dimple time, make time a vortex,
Suck time backward through itself, and
We return through its forward going:

We, by mercy, pass its latter sadness first; we
Meet its middle as our own, most penitential;
We arrive then at its first, the simplex,
Our last home and holing.

This is the marvel of our celebration
And the grace of God:
To take us back
Through headlong time,
To make us small
And tuck us home
Again.

O baby, rest your nappy head;
Your eyes be rollin', you half dead;
Your mama loves you, wide and deep—
O baby, baby, steal to sleep:
   Your story's done
     Begun

6. A Quiet Chamber Kept for Thee

This is the way it was in the old days:

The milkman still delivered milk to our back door, summer and winter; the milk came in bottles, and the bottles were shaped with a bulge at the top for the cream, you see, which separated after the milk was bottled. Cream was common, in those days. So was butter. Margarine was less appealing because, according to Canadian law, it had to be sold in its original color, which was white like lard, and could be colored yellow only by the customer after she had bought it. Or so my mother told me. She mixed an orange powder into the margarine to make it butter–yellow.

But this is the way it was in the old days:

The milkman still drove a horse-drawn wagon, arriving at our house in the middle of the morning. And especially in the winter we would, as my mother said, "tune our ears to hear his coming." That is, we listened for the kindly, congregational clinking of the glass in his wagon as he toiled down our particular street, then we rushed to an upstairs window and watched. In the cold Canadian air, you could hear his coming from far away. We were breathing on the window long before the milkman came bustling up our walk with bottles in a wire basket. And that, of course, was the point: my mother wanted us to bring the milk in right away, or else it would freeze and the cream would lift its hat on an ice-cream column: "How-do-you-do?" "Fine, thank you, Cream, and how are you?"

But this is the way it was especially on Christmas Eve Day:

We spent the major portion of the morning at that upstairs window, giggling, whispering, and waiting for the milkman to come. Tradition. My mother was glad to be shed of us on the day she "ran crazy" with preparations. I think we knew that then. But for our own part, we did truly want to see some evidence of how cold it was outside. It was important that Christmas Eve be cold. And it was the milkman's mare, you see, who presented us with evidence.

So here came the mare in a slow walk, nodding, drawing the wagon behind her even when her master was rushing up sidewalks, making deliveries. She never stopped. And the mare was blowing plumes of steam from her nostrils. Her chin had grown a beard of hoarfrost. Her back was blanketed. The blanket smoked. The air was cold. The air was very cold, and our stomachs contracted with joy within us, and some of us laughed at the rightness of the weather. So here came the mare, treading a hardened snow. The snow banked six feet high on either side of the street, except at sidewalks and driveways; the snow was castles we would be kings of tomorrow. The snow collected on the mare, whose forelock and eyelashes were white. She shivered the flesh on her flanks, sending off small showers of snow; and so did we—shiver. Ah, cold! The air was a crystal bowl of cold! The day was perfectly right.

And we could scarcely stand the excitement.

Downstairs, directly below us in the house, was a room that had been locked two days ago against our entering in. This was my father's tradition, which he never varied year to year. Always, he locked the door by removing its knob, transfiguring thereby the very spirit of the room; all we could do was spy at the knob-hole and wonder at the mysteries concealed inside. My brothers and sisters pestered that hole continually, chirping among themselves like snowbirds on a holly tree, puffing their imaginations like feathers all around them.

Tonight, on Christmas Eve itself, we would all line up, and my father would slip the knob back into the door, and one by one we would enter the wondrous room. This much we knew: the Christmas tree was in there.

Therefore, even in the morning at the upstairs window, we could scarcely stand the excitement.

Tonight! And lo: it was very, very cold.

Let me be more specific. We were living in Edmonton, Alberta, then. The year was 1954, and I was ten, the oldest of seven children. I've implied that we were all excited on that particular Christmas Eve morning, and so we were; but though my brothers and sisters could manifest their excitement with unbridled delight, I could not mine. I absolutely refused to acknowledge or signal excitement. They loved the sweet contractions in their stomachs. I was afraid of them. For I had that very year become an adult: silent, solemn, watchful, and infinitely cautious.

So my brothers and sisters laughed and clapped the day away. They spilled colored sugar on cookie dough and covered the kitchen table with a sweet mess, all unworried, unafraid. They claimed, by faster stabs of the finger, their individual treasures from Sears catalogues, and so they allowed their dreams to soar, and so they passed the day. I didn't blame them. They were innocent; they could dare the dangers they didn't see. These children could rush headlong toward the evening, recklessly. But I could not.

I held myself in a severe restraint. Because—what if you hope, and it doesn't happen? It's treacherous to hope. The harder you hope, the more vulnerable you become. And what if you believe a thing, but it isn't true? Well, the instant you see the deception, you die a little. And it hurts exactly in your soul, where once you had believed. I knew all this. I had learned that excitement is composed of hope and faith together—but of faith and hope in promises yet unkept—and I was not about to let excitement run away with me, or I would certainly crash as I had crashed the year before.

Last Christmas Eve, in the midst of opening his presents,

my brother Paul had burst into tears. I didn't know—and I don't know—why. But I was shocked to discover that the Christmas time was not inviolate. I was horrified that pain could invade the holy ceremony. And I was angry that my father had not protected my brother from tears. There was a fraud here. The traditions were as thin as a crystal globe and empty. I could do nothing about that when I was nine years old, nothing but sob in sympathy with my brother, nothing but grieve to the same degree that I had believed.

But by ten I was an adult; and if Christmas gave me nothing really, and if the traditions could not protect me from assault, then I would protect myself.

No: the more excited I was, the more I was determined not to be, and the more I molded my face into a frown.

I'm speaking with precision now. None of us could stand the season's excitement. But I was frightened by mine and chose to show it to no one, not to my father, not to my mother, and not to myself.

Adult.

By supper the world was black outside, so the noise inside seemed louder than it had been, and we the closer together. In bathrobes we ate soup. We had bathed: bright faces, soft faces, sparkling eyes in faces glowing with their goodness. Children smile with a self-conscious piety on Christmas Eve, nearly drowning in convictions of their goodness. My brothers and sisters ran to their bedrooms, bubbling, and began to dress themselves.

I stood before the bathroom mirror and combed my hair with water, unsmiling.

Always we went to church on Christmas Eve to participate in the children's service. Nothing happened at home till after that. This was the tradition; and tradition itself began when we would venture into the cold, cold night, on our way to perform the parts we had been practicing for endless Saturdays. And if we were nervous about the lines we had to say, well, that only intensified excitement for the time thereafter, the room, the mystery, and the tree.

My hair froze as soon as I walked outside. It crackled when I touched it. It felt like a cap. Cold. My face tightened in the night wind, and I blew ghosts of steam that the wind took from my lips. They were leaving me and wouldn't come back again.

The family sat three, three, and three in the three seats of a VW van, I in the farthest corner of the back, slouched, my hands stuffed in my pockets. I forced myself to repeat my lines for the pageant. I was to be Isaiah.

So then it was a blazing church we crowded into, a small church filled with yellow light and stifling excitement. People were laughing simply at the sight of one another, as though familiar faces were a fine hilarity: "You, Harold, ha-ha-ha, *you!* Well, Merry Christmas to you!" In the narthex the press of people squashed us because we wore thick coats; and the children were shooed downstairs to giddy into costumes, and the adults clumped upstairs to wait in pews, and holly greens were knocked from the windowsills, and the windows were black with night. Who is so foolish as to laugh in such an atmosphere and not to fear that he's losing control? Not me.

Class by class the children trooped into the chancel. As the pageant proceeded they sang with wide-open mouths all full of faith, eyes unafraid. The little ones waved to their parents by the crooking of four fingers, like scratching air. They positively shined with happiness. No one thought to be fearful.

I, in my turn, stared solemnly at the massed congregation and intoned, "For unto us a child is born, unto us a son." I saw the adults jammed shoulder to shoulder in ranks before me, nodding and craning, encouraging me by grins, not a whit afraid. "Wonderful, Counsellor—" No one was ready to cry in the midst of so much cheer and danger. Naive people—or else they were cunning. Well, neither would I. "Mighty God!" I roared. I would not cry. Neither would I succumb to the grins of these parents, no. "Everlasting Father!" Oh, no, I would not risk disappointment again this year. "The Prince of Peace!" I thundered, and I quit. No emotion whatsoever. I did not laugh. I did not smile. Both of these are treacherous. I made a glowering prophet altogether. My father and mother sat nearly hidden ten rows back. I noticed them just before descending from the chancel.

Walnuts, tangerines, a curled rock candy all in a small brown bag—and every kid got a bag at the end of the service. A bag was thrust toward me, and I took it, but I didn't giggle and I didn't open it. *No sir! You won't entice me to gladness or gratitude.*

And the people, humping into coats again, called, "Merry Christmas! Merry Christmas!"—the pleasant tumult of departure. They were flowing outward into the black night, tossing goodwill over their shoulders: "Merry Christmas!" *No, ma'am! You won't disarm me again this year.*

Even now my father delayed our going home. Tradition. As long as I can remember, my father found ways to while the time, increasing excitement until his children fairly panted piety and almost swooned in their protracted goodness.

"Don't breathe through your noses," my father sang out, hunched at the wheel of the van. This was his traditional joke. "You'll steam the windows. Breathe through your ears," he called.

Silliness. We breathed through our noses anyway, frosting the windows a quarter-inch thick, enclosing our family in a cave of space in the night. With mittened hands and elbows we rubbed peepholes through the muzzy ice. We were driving through the city to view its Christmas decorations, lights and trees and stables and beasts and effigies of the Holy Family. This, too, was tradition.

I looked out my little hole and regarded the scenes with melancholy.

There was a tremendous tableau of Dickensian carolers in

someone's yard, some dozen people in tall hats and scarves and muffs, their mouths wide open, their eyes screwed up to heaven in a transport of song—their bodies a wooden fiction. They didn't move. They didn't produce a note of music. So: nobody heard them. But nobody minded. Because no one was singing. And no living body was anywhere near them anyway.

This was worse than silliness. This was dangerous. I found myself suddenly full of pity for the wooden figures, as though they could be lonely in the deserted snow. Any feeling at all made me vulnerable. I stopped looking.

My boots crunched snow when we walked to the door of our house. A wind with crystals caused my eyes to tear. But resolutely, I was not crying.

And still my father delayed our going into the room.

Oh, who could control the spasms of his excitement? Oh, Dad! Let's *do* it and be done with it!

But it was tradition, upon returning home, that we change our church clothes into pajamas, and gather in the kitchen.

Across the hall the door was still closed—but its knob had been replaced. I saw that knob, and my heart kicked inside of me. So I chewed my bottom lip and frowned like thunder: *No! It won't be what it ought to be. It never is.*

Adult.

And always, always the hoops of my father's tradition: we lined up in the kitchen from the youngest to the oldest. I stood last in a line of seven. My littlest sister was clasping her hands and raising her shining, saintly face to my father, who stood before her facing us. Her hair hung down her back to the waist. Blithe child! Her blue eyes burst with trust. I pitied her.

My father prayed a prayer, tormenting me. For the prayer evoked the very images I was refusing: infant Jesus, gift of God, love come down from heaven—all of the things that conspired to make me glad at Christmas. My poor heart bucked and disputed that prayer. No! I would not hope. No! I would not permit excitement. No! No! I would not be set up for a second disappointment.

We were a single minute from entering the room.

And I might have succeeded at severity—

—except that then we sang a song, the same song we had always sung, and the singing undid me altogether. Music destroys me. A hymn will reduce me to infancy.

Nine bare voices, unaccompanied in the kitchen, we sang: *Ah, dearest Jesus, holy child*—and I began to tremble. —*Make thee a bed, soft, undefiled*— The very sweetness of the melody caused my defenses to fall: I began to hope, and I began to fear, both at once. I began to wish, and wishing made me terrified. I began all over again to believe, but I had never ceased my unbelief. I began to panic. —*Within my heart; that it may be*— Dreadfully, now, I yearned for some good thing to be found in that room, but "dreadfully," I say, because I was an adult; I'd put away the childish things; I'd been disillusioned and knew no good to be in there. This was a pitiless sham!

—*A quiet chamber kept for thee.*

My father whispered, "Now."

He turned to the door.

Little squeals escaped my sister.

He grasped the knob and opened the door upon a muted, colored light; and one by one his children crept through the door and into that room.

All of his children save one. I lingered in the doorway, looking, not breathing.

There, shedding a dim and varied light, was the Christmas tree my father had decorated alone, every single strand of tinsel hanging straight down of its own slim weight, since he hung them individually, patiently, and would not hasten the duty by tossing them in fistfuls (tradition!)—the tree he had hidden three days ago behind a knobless door.

There, in various places about the room, were seven piles of gifts, a pile for each of us.

There, in the midst of them, my mother sat smiling on the floor, her skirts encircling her, her own radiance smiting my eyes, for she verged on laughter. My mother always laughed when she gave presents, however long the day had been before, however crazy she had almost gone. I began to blink rapidly.

But there, unaccountably, was my father, standing center in the room and gazing straight at me. At me. And this is the wonder fixed in my memory: that the man himself was filled with a yearning, painful expectation; but that he, like me, was withholding still his own excitement—on account of *me.*

Everything else in this room was just as it had been the year before, and the year before that. But this was new. This thing I had never seen before: that my father, too, had passed his day in the hope that risks a violent hurt. My father, too, had had to trust the promises against their disappointments. So said his steady eyes on me. But among the promises to which my father had committed his soul, his hope and his faith, the most important one was this: that his eldest son should soften and be glad.

If I had grown adult in 1954, then lo, how like a child my father had become! The colored lights painted the side of his face. He gazed at me, waiting, waiting for me, waiting for his Christmas to be received by his son and returned to him again.

And I began to cry. O my father!

Silently, merely spilling the tears and staring straight back at him, defenseless because there was no need for defenses, I cried—glad and unashamed. Because, what was this room, for so long locked, which I was entering? Why, it was my own heart. And why had I been afraid? Because I thought I'd find it empty, a hard, unfeeling thing.

But there, in the room, was my father.

And there, in my father, was the love that had furnished this room, preparing it for us no differently than he had last year prepared it, yet trusting and yearning, desiring our joy.

And what else could such a love be, but my Jesus drawing near?

Look, then, what I have found in my father's room, in my heart after all: the dearest Lord Jesus, holy child—

The nativity of our Lord.

I leaned my cheek against the doorjamb and grinned like a grown-up ten years old, and sobbed as if I were two. And my father moved from the middle of the room and walked toward me, still empty-handed; but he spread his hands and gathered me to himself. And I put my arms around his harder body. And so we, both of us, were full.

This is the way that it was in the olden days.

7. Wherefore White

For that the lily *candidum,* Madonna's lily, when it opens to the daily Gabriel of the sun, is white; and it is good, as God did, still to start with Mary: *Ave gratia plena—*

For that virginity, awaiting yet its script, some word, the Word to make a sense of it, hath ever been as white as an unwritten sheet: but God sends purpose to the possibilities. *Hail, thou greatly favored one—*

For that the Holy Spirit, coming low to overshadow her, if it had visibility at all, was whiter than the piling cloud: it was a vapor of the Deity, it was a wind, the breath of God—

For that humility is colorless and purity its shining; and these Maria was when *Ecce* said: said, *Ecce ancilla Domini,* I, the hand-maid of the Lord; said humbly to the messenger of God, *Fiat!* Let it be!—

For that the snow, which sometimes cloaks this season, cover-ing the parti-colored tantrums of humanity in one hue only, cool and smooth, is white—

For that white is all the colors in chromatic harmony, precise equality: the fusion of unity; and there was one babe, one God above us—

For that white is the innocence of the Infant, the nimbus wheeling round his face—

For that the glory that shone around the shepherds was un-quenchable, a white flame from the throne of God—

For that all the stars did next throw down their spears, take up a canticle, and sing above the midnight of the shepherds; and these, the multitude of the heavenly host, were white—

For that their song was *Et in terra, pax!* Peace! was the pleading of the stars; peace! concluded their doxology: Peace to the people with whom he is pleased. And the figure of peace is a dove. And the dove is white—

For that if wars should cease on one day, the next day's dawning would be white as fleece—

For that the holy deed remembered in this season admits of no division, none other instrument than God's pure love alone, no human help, though humans have the benefit: the only-begotten Son was a gift from the Father of Lights, with whom there is no variation nor shadow due to changing, white—

For that the eyes of all are whiter than the skins of any—

For that I cried, when I knelt down with treasures for the child, a single tear, and lo: my tear meant more to him than myrrh; which tear he touched and turned to coal; which tear he took, now blacker than his pupil, and wore against his breast; but then he sank from sight beneath the earth, and so the age and all humanity were heaped upon him. But when he rose again, I saw my tear rise with him, and behold: it was a diamond, white at the heart of it—

For that the teeth of children when they laugh are ivory, and their laughter is a pearl—

—Therefore at the Christmastide we drape our holy furniture and stole the necks of those who preach in white.

8. A Minor Revelation

I looked, and behold: a door was opened in heaven.

And an enormous voice, like many waters falling, was talking with me, saying, "Come up hither. I've a minor revelation which, afterward, you may record in a minor volume, if you have the faith that one or two might listen—"

Immediately I was lightsome in the spirit. And, as insubstantial as imagination, I crept, mere nothing, into the heavenly places. Behold: a blinding throne. And listen: a rolling, booming conversation which, having the faith required, I set before you now.

Then where are my one or two? Where is the poor heart, yearning from her poverty? And the humiliated heart made hungry by that same humiliation for a kinder word and righteousness?

Come. Listen. Those who have hears to hear, let them hear—that lilies only look like trumpets. . . .

It was furnished like a courtroom—or like the wide sky with white, columnar clouds massed at the four corners. In the center rose a judge's dais of innumerable steps—or else it was a mountain. And he who sat thereon, in the midst of an impossible light, was speaking.

"Again, Gabriel," said the voice in the light. "Do it again."

I looked and saw an angel standing on the air. He held in his hand an unsealed scroll, darkened on both sides with much writing, and he wore a darker frown upon his face. He hesitated, saying nothing, frowning, but doing nothing.

The voice of God said, "Gabriel?"

Then the angel bowed down, down before the shining Deity until his frown fell black upon the earth below, like shadow; and I heard him speak.

He said, still bowing, "Do you mind if I take my trumpet this time?" His frown was the storm that threatens in the distance, his breath the prairie wind. "How," he said, "if I give them a little toot?" His eyes forked lightning where he looked. People rushed indoors.

But the voice of God said, "Ah, Gabriel. Not yet, Gabriel."

The angel said, "Neither one of us is blind."

The voice of God said, "Thank you for the company."

The angel rumbled, "See? See? Let me blow a blast for what we see."

"We'll keep the trumpet," said the voice of God, "for another time. Just go and do what you've done before, as well and as gracefully as ever you have done it—"

"Useless!" boomed the angel, rising suddenly to a full celestial height and staring boldly into brilliance. "I tell you," he thundered—and doors slammed shut all over the earth and windows closed and, verily, people huddled in their basements—"I tell you, sir, it doesn't work!"

But the great light blazed upon its throne, scorching the eyebrows of the angel and causing him to squint. "Did I ask you to assess the probabilities?" demanded the voice of the Almighty God. "Did I request opinions?"

But the angel set his jaw and gathered his robes around him. "Begging your pardon, Highness," he muttered thunder, trying hard to seem subservient yet consumed with righteousness, "I know you know and I do not—the nature of things, and so forth; the great chain of being never to be disputed, and so forth. But sir! I have gone this route before, one-thousand-nine-hundred-and-fifty times before, ever declaring the same good news. And according to my estimate (admittedly incomplete, though I *am* an archangel, after all, by thine own appointment) there has been a singular lack of change among the people through the centuries. On the other hand, it is marvelous to see how moved they are by *bad* news, those so hardened to the good. The trumpet—"

"And you, dear Gabriel, by *my* irrefutable estimate," said

the voice upon the throne, "have argued this same case before me one-thousand-nine-hundred-and-forty-nine times. I am a patient Deity—"

"Patient! Patient! *Too* patient altogether!" roared the angel, cracked and raged and boomed the exasperated angel. Cattle put their backs to a rising wind. Cities went silent in their dread. The trees were whipped until the air was filled with leaves and wild limbs. It was eerie to see the storm and the sun together in the sky. People considered praying.

For a moment the voice of God did not answer, allowing divine silence alone to shame an angel his impetuosities.

Perhaps the stillness of God is greater chastening than the voice of him speaking, and harder to endure. The angel Gabriel controlled himself, folded his arms, pressed the scroll against his chest, and besought another avenue of argument. When he spoke again, he'd reduced his voice to reason, which was a low, persistent rumble above the earth.

"Listen, this is the way that it was," he said. "The first time round I told the ladies that the Son had risen. I, with smiling expectations for the wonder and the holiness of a thing absolutely miraculous, and glad that you had chosen me, I delivered the message. The ladies," he said, "told the apostles, who straightway mounted a campaign to tell the world; and the world (to my amazement, human voices being nothing next to hark-the-herald-angels' song) was told indeed. And then what? But *then* what happened upon the broadcasting of such good news?"

The angel paused for effect.

The Deity, knowing all things, did not answer.

The people below peeped out of their doors, wondering whether their prayers had been heard and if the storm was passing after all.

"Nothing!" snapped the angel.

Crack! went the thunder in heaven.

And *bang, bang, bang,* doors shut all over the earth again, and people cursed the indecision of divinities.

"Nothing happened," said the angel. "Nothing, except that my eyes were opened to the human nature—"

"Let an archangel," said the voice of the Lord, quietly, "open his eyes to *my* nature—"

"—to the human nature, I say, which has not in two millennia disappointed me or changed. Ah, sir. Ah, sir, but I have changed. This year, weary with the useless repetition," said the angel, loosening his scroll and blackening the sky by the length of it and panicking the people below—for darkness at noon must surely presage the end of things—"this year I have kept a list, simply to forestall another futile attempt on our part."

I looked, and behold: the scroll extended from one end of heaven to the other, as though it were the sky rolled back, and the writing seemed a galaxy of dark stars, and the people gave up prayer in their despair, and the angel began to read from it, and the doom of his voice fell everywhere at once upon the whole sphere of the earth.

"Wars," he read, "continual, in which none are unrighteous and none are monstrous, but every side considers itself justified and for this reason deploys artilleries unthinkable but sleeps at peace with its soul; wars uncountable, whose blood and money are not reserved to the combatants alone, but kill the children, kill the children, too; wars perpetual—"

"The Lord," whispered the Lord in light, "the Lord God, merciful and gracious—"

"—divorces," Gabriel read on, unhearing. "Three billion, six hundred and twenty-four million, seven thousand and two counts of adultery, and the babies born of these are unloved and unprotected, particularly by the fathers, and young mothers know no way to raise them purely. Manipulated prices by management, strikes by labor (the sin begets its sin). Thefts by consumers who feel a life is owed to them—"

"—long-suffering," whispered the Lord in light, "abundant in goodness and truth—"

"—Murders of myriad variety, for the human heart is creative; murders boring in their repetition, for their causes and their consequences are always the same, though each considers itself unique. Pride so high it offends the sky. Gossip more cunning than their poets could compose—"

"—keeping mercy for thousands—"

"—Poverty on purpose. Injustice, injustice, let me see, injustice (this seems a universal practice). Plain, brutish, yet self-justified racism. Child abuse, together with the companion habit of dishonoring parents. The beatings of those one promised to love forever—"

"—forgiving iniquity and transgression and sin. Gabriel—"

"—Gluttony, especially in the West, which, with laziness, insults obscenely the bodies you created—"

"Gabriel!" cried the Lord.

"What?" The archangel looked up, not half through.

"Look at me."

"I can barely see you."

"Look at me!" commanded the voice in light, and the light swelled brighter and brighter, blinding heaven and making coals of the angel's eyes. Smoke rolled forth. A celestial flame began to race the edges of the scroll, and the people were confused by what seemed cataclysm in the sky, for the storm threatened and threatened; it hove above, but it did not break nor drop.

"I've heard your list," roared the voice of the Lord in a visible whirlwind, "and you've heard mine; but which of us can hold his list in the infinities? Which endures? Which, dear Gabriel?"

Suddenly the scroll exploded into fire, and heaven glowed a violent orange, and a yellow wind shrieked, and the poor archangel clung to his scroll as to a whipping sail, muttering, "Well. Well. Well, but—"

But the fire—no common fire, a fire supernal, reserved for Sinais and theophanies—the fire swept toward him too; and when it began to scorch his hands, the angel let go. He couldn't hold the accusing thing. He covered his face. And

burning, burning, then, the scroll arose in heaven like a float-
ing, flaming robe, spreading color from the west even unto the
east: saffron, red, vermillion, crimson, purple, and the cooler
blue.

The people crept outside their houses, gazing upward and
uttering bleats of relief. "Why," they said to one another,
astonished that they could have been so foolish, "why, it was
only a sunset and no storm!" They sighed. They giggled, the
little people did. They congratulated themselves that the
world was the same after all, nothing changed, nobody truly
endangered, no destruction come near to them, no reason to
be afraid. Or to pray.

And the angel Gabriel was humbled. He sank to his knees
upon the air and lowered his face.

But the Lord God, out of an evening glory, consoled him.

"Gabriel, Gabriel," whispered the Lord like the zephyr, the
west wind. "Gabriel, your list was about them and for yourself—for yourself, if even only for your love of righteousness.
It could not last. It had an ending in its very nature. It *concerned*
death. But my list is about me and for them. It shall endure
as long as I shall choose it to. I *am* life. People were the
substance of your list: poor pence, poor Gabriel, if the list is
to be entered into the assizes. They'll kill you. But I am the
substance of mine: I *am* the assizes. And I choose mercy one
more time—to let them live.

"Oh, don't try to reason it, angel mine." The tone of the
Almighty was gentle, softened by laughter. "It is perfectly
unreasonable."

Again I looked, and behold: the deepening light upon its
throne upon its mountaintop grew and grew in a milder manner. It enveloped the angel Gabriel wholly, kindly. An angel
chastened, an angel empty, he was both filled and surrounded
by the brightness of God, and so he disappeared to my sight.
Then it seemed to me that I was alone in the heavenly places;
and, strangely, I felt a catch in my throat as though suddenly
I might weep. I could not, like the people on the earth, lie

down in the night to sleep serenely now: for I had been
granted the revelation. I had been made a restless creature.

But then, out of the twilight glowing on the mountaintop,
I heard the voice of God again, in love with his messenger:
"Gabriel, go. Descend, dear angel, one more time. Find some
shepherd willing to cry the truth out one more time—that they
are forgiven your list, that they need not die in the squalid
condition of their lives."

Find some shepherd. Ah, immediately I prayed that it might be
me.

"The trumpet," said the Lord in royal light, "is for the day
when I cease to say, 'Once more, go down once more.' The
trumpet shall fix them forever. But today there's still some
change I seek. Some turning. Some warmer flicker of faith—"

Then I rushed to be found in the body when Gabriel would
come down without the trumpet, crying, "Good tidings! Good
tidings!" I hastened among the churches searching the shepherd who took the tune to sing it too: "Good tidings! Good
tidings!" I beat on the doors of the people, a shepherd myself,
declaring, "Good tidings!"

And I have written it in a minor volume breathlessly: Good
tidings, good people—one more time.

ORDINARY TIME:
The Seasons Green

9.   Mary, Just Eleven

I watched you swimming, Mary. You were as unconscious of me as you were of yourself; but I was exquisitely aware of you, and then of myself as well.

Mary! You're not a woman yet, but womanhood is in you.

And suddenly, by slow degrees, the quality of my fatherhood is changing: new demands upon my soul, new dangers, revelations, new moments of the primeval quiet—and sometimes I'm a mumblin' fool with you, and sometimes I gaze in wonder like Balboa when he stood on an escarpment and stared at the Pacific.

Mary, what are you doing to me?

What is happening to you?

The changes come slowly, to be sure; but we poor parents wake to them as though in surprise, and then we seek sympathy from companion parents, some consolation for the bewildering transformations of our children—while you children sometimes seem to take the whirling world so easily that we feel Paleolithic beside you. Sometimes, I say. For there are times when your limber spirit stiffens and brittles and breaks, and then you are like a figurine shattered, and no one can glue you, no, no one can put you together again.

Yesterday I watched you swimming in a blue Wisconsin lake—you, seabird, all alone. I sat some twenty feet above you on a bluff and so could see Olympian, as it were, could see through the lake to its bed below you, whose stones you never touched: you stroked too well and lightly through the element. Child, you were delightful, flicking the water like a trout with liquid, familiar assurance—

But then I caught my breath and leaned forward, the better to see: Mary! Your legs are so long! And strong. And they churned the water with luxurious competence. And the crystal water gave them a pale, aquatic cast—dreamlike, it seemed to me, and absolutely beautiful. Mary! When did you come to be so beautiful? There are true hips at the ascendant curve of those legs, and a slender waist where once a child threw out her belly, and brown and lithesome arms, and bold shoulders. And when you toweled yourself, your wet lashes joined together like black starbursts, radiating glory round your eyes—blue eyes, shooting lashes, and a laughing child! Oh, Mary, when did you come to be so beautiful?

And when did you begin to stop to be a child?

When did the woman commence, whom only now I notice?

All at once! By slow degrees.

There was a period, five or six years ago, when your older brothers received more letters than usual from aunts and uncles who addressed them in formal terms: "Master" Joseph and "Master" Matthew Wangerin. Talitha was perplexed by a title she had never heard before.

"If boys are masters," your younger sister said, "then what are girls?"

You solved it straightway, as easy as swimming.

"Masterpieces!" you declared.

And mom laughed at the aptness, since you are a piece of work; and I laughed for three or four seasons; and you—you laughed for the pure pink pleasure of it all, the center of attention, a round cheesecake of a child, dumpling cheeks, not a cloud in your blue sky.

Well, now in these latter weeks I realize, sweet Mary, variations in that laughter. The weather's less stable than it used to be, isn't it?—and could change upon the instant.

Oh, the laughter's eager still; you grin so hard, and your eyes desire to swallow the one you're laughing with, and you clasp your hands at your breast (like any Jane Austen, I think, or any Victorian) never, never to let the sweet sensation go—

But suddenly, now, a single word can change your aspect altogether. One frown from another can collapse the happi-

ness and spill true tears down cheeks still formed for grinning.
And the harder you laugh these days, the likelier are these
tears. High and low emotions are one with you, exultation and
despair: you take offense as quickly as the snail's horn, and
then my offended daughter, with her long, strong woman's
legs, runs up the stairsteps wailing (a Victorian perfection of
grammar), "You do not understand! No one understands me!
I could just die—" And the bedroom door slams for punctua-
tion, and you sail (in a graceful trajectory, I am sure) through
the air and to your bed of bitterness, weeping. "I could just
die."

A woman you are, a woman of complicated (I'm serious
about that), intense, and deep emotions. No, you are not
acting. This isn't a pretence. Nor do you try on moods as
people try on dresses to buy. The moods are painfully real in
you, and life is less simple than it was. Relationships for you
are in fact divine. Or else disastrous. And the divinity or the
damage *does* last forever, until tomorrow. (Again, I'm serious;
I am not teasing you, my daughter: today is forever in your
baby woman's heart, and tomorrow is ever your wonder, un-
expected when it doth come.)

A woman you are. But to me what are you, Mary?

My lover. (Oh, yes!) You comfort me in a manner most
mature, having learned since childhood to read my moody
meditations. Your eyes are perceptive. You see me truly, and
quick to the heart; and your hand consoles me, even when
lightly you pass in the kitchen and pause in the passing; and
you are beautiful in compassion. A woman. Such a woman.

But what are you to me?

A thunderstorm! A headache. (Oh, yes! So changeth the
weather.) Suddenly things are not hard for you, not merely
difficult: they are *"impossible,* Father!" Anything I ask you to
do, when you're convinced that you cannot or should not or
will not do it, causes you trauma—and formalizes me in the
process, refusing me my more intimate names and freezing
me with "Father." Then how do I reason with one who de-

clares with creedal conviction that I "hate" her? One tormented by loneliness, lovelessness, as forlorn as the poet at the fading of his nightingale? One who sees me as the Ogre, the Ancient, both stony and hateful, the Judge, the Warden, and the Executioner?

I don't. I'm smarter than that. (I learned from my father.) I do not try to reason with such a one. Simply: I wait for tomorrow, which, though you dispute the turning of the times, shall most surely come. I wait for tomorrow, when I shall be your intimate again, and your only friend.

Ah, Mary, when did you begin to stop to be a child? It's a difficult business, isn't it, this adulthood. You yearn it and you curse it, woman.

When did you begin to cover yourself and lock the bathroom door against us? When did you begin to take yourself and all the world (and right and wrong, and justice and injustice) so seriously? And when did you become so beautiful?

All at once! By creeping, slow degrees.

God gave us a sky of infinite and wild variety, storms and the imperial blue, scudding clouds and the symphonic sunset and lightning too. But the sky never touched me lightly to say, "I love you." Nor could that sky receive my little love in return.

So God gave us daughters—
—more wonderful than the sky, lights for telling the seasons by.

Ah, Mary.

Masterpiece!

10. A Hymn in Ordinary Time

Signs! Signs! A singular star
  Outblazing constellations
Inscribed the sky in this regard:
  "A King for all the nations."
  The Magi read the word,
    And found the Lord,
    And found the Lord.

Signs! Signs! A thundering dove
  Descended to creation,
Itself a symbol, Sacred Love,
  Its cry a consecration:
  "Beloved Son, with Thee
    Am I well pleased,
    Am I well pleased."

Signs! Signs! Consignments of wine
  Surpassing sixty gallon
Renewed a wedding in decline
  When lesser spirits failed them.
  And who had done this? Who?
    Disciples knew.
    Disciples knew.

Signs! Signs! A face was inflamed,
  The noonday sun descending;
Both Moses and Elijah came;
  The cloud cried out, commending
  To Peter, James, and John
    "A Son, my Son,
    Beloved One!"

Signs! Signs! The world is a book,
  And what is not the writing?
The world is charged, for them that look,
  With grandeur; God's reminding,
  In all things near to thee,
    To read and see
    Divinity.
  And signs explode for thee
    Epiphanies,
    Epiphanies.

11. The Farmer at Eighty-Eight

It's cold. The ground is frozen now. A light snow has dusted it, which shall be some moisture if the weather relents and lets it melt before it simply evaporates. It's winter, now, after a terrible season of heat and drought. Scientists surmise that we ourselves may be responsible for the enmity of the weather, that we have unbalanced its delicate, interdependent elements, the ordered exchange of energies. They suggest that headlong technology creates a waste, which the environment cannot process.

I am no scientist. I attend to the spirit of the people rather more than to their engineering skills, mechanical expertise. I weigh and evaluate the spirit rather better than I can empirical phenomena.

Nevertheless, to the scientist, sadly I say, "Yes. It is possible." Possible, and given the power, it is likely. The spirit of this race is fully capable of the sin that does not love its own environment, but makes of itself a god to be satisfied, and makes of the earth a sacrifice the gods devour. The spirit of this race is well able to justify the slaughter—first because it doesn't confess that the earth is alive, so there was no slaughter in the first place; second because it has made a morality of its economics, has made of its money a *summum bonum,* and is more concerned for the healthy flow of cash than the healthy, regenerative flow of rivers and streams.

The race, did I say? No, not all of the race. Those presently in power, perhaps; but not everyone lacks humility and reverence. Therein is hope.

Chief Seattle might have laughed at the thought that anyone could buy or sell the earth. But because the fool who thought so also had the power to enforce his folly, Chief Seattle didn't laugh. Rather, he grieved. And he wrote a letter.

He wrote: "If we sell you our land, you must keep it sacred, a place where even the white man can taste the wind that is sweetened by the meadow's flowers." Did anyone who read his letter suppose that Chief Seattle was being merely poetical? Romantic, maybe? Irrelevant, surely, to the harder facts of life.

He wrote: "This shining water that moves in the streams and rivers is not just water but the blood of our ancestors. You must teach your children that it is sacred. If we sell you our land, you must teach your children that the rivers are your brothers, and you must henceforth give the rivers the kindness you would give any brother." Does anyone who reads his letter today suppose that Chief Seattle is speaking merely symbolically? That his notions are primitive? That they are suspect, moreover, because they sound distinctly pagan? Does the following sound pagan—or anything but spiritually righteous and pragmatically self-evident?

He wrote: "The earth does not belong to man; man belongs to the earth. Whatever befalls the earth befalls the sons of the earth"—befalls the children of Adam, whose very name remembers that from which he was made: clay, dirt, soil, earth, ground. "If men spit on the earth," wrote Chief Seattle of the Duwamish League of Puget Sound in 1854 to the United States Government in the East, "they spit on themselves. All things are connected."

And what shall I say? That his prophecy frightens me?

I will say: His grieving gives me hope.

But what shall I say? That he lived too long ago? That his insights are estranged from us, being the vision of an Indian, another race, an alien and defeated nation?

No. I will say: The vision is living still, even in those who are near to me, yes, intimate to me and thee.

Therein is hope.

All the hot, dry summer long I've thought of my father-in-law, who was a farmer until he retired, who never owned the land he worked but who loved it. The soil was holy, and he knew it.

My wife remembers her childhood, when her father plowed behind two draft horses. They were steady beasts with hooves the size of her head. It frightened the little girl to lead them to water, to walk between these engines of bone and rolling hide, because the quicker she ran, the faster they took their giant strides, and she feared she couldn't stop them when they came to the trough, however loud she shrieked.

But her father commanded them mutely and absolutely—a gesture, a cluck, a tap of the bridle. Silent farmer. Silent, stolid horses. He used them still when neighbors were driving tractors. They were a living companionable power. His was a holy union with them, and he knew it.

Martin Bohlmann was born with the century. He's eighty-eight years old.

Horses pulled his mower. There was a time when horses pulled the rake that laid the alfalfa in windrows to dry—and then his fields were drawn in long, strong lines of a darker green, like emotion in an ancient face.

When the hay was dry, the horses pulled a flat wagon slowly down the windrows, and one man forked the hay to another standing on the wagon. The second man caught the bundles neatly with his own fork and flicked them down into an intricate cross-arrangement, building a pile of hay and climbing his work as he did, building the pile so tight, so high, that when the horses pulled the wagon to the barn, the man on his haystack could stare dead-level into the second-story windows of the farmhouse.

Horses pulled the rope that, over a metal wheel, hoisted hay to the barn loft. They made hayricks of the overflow and covered the ricks with tarpaulins staked to the ground, or else they thatched the tops of the ricks. The work caused a dust, and the dust caused a fearful itch and put grit in his teeth on a sweating summer's day. But the work and the hay—the fodder for fall and the winter to come—were holy. Martin Bohlmann knew that.

He milked the cows before the sunrise. There was a time when he sat on a stool with his cheek against a warm flank in the winter; and the scent in his nostrils was richer than soil, was pungent with the life of beasts; and he heard, in the caverns of the cow, wind, the deeper roaring of her breathing. The cow would swing her head around to gaze at him with one brown eye, luxuriant lashes. He pinched the teats in the joint of his thumb and squeezed with the rest of his hand: a ringing *spritz* hit the pail between his feet. Then tug by tug, with needle-shots of a blue-white milk, he filled the pail, and the sound of the squirts was a plunking. Sometimes he aimed a squirt at the cat who lived in the barn. Then he rose and sloshed the milk from pail to can. Then he carried the cans outside.

The winter air had a marvelous bite after the warmth of the barn. The farmer's boots would squeak on the snow as he lugged full cans to the milkhouse. The dawn was grey at the eastern horizon, so the sky seemed huge and deep, and the white earth ghostly still. *Crack* went the ice in the distance. *Crack* went the great limbs of the trees. Someone might say that the farmer alone in his yard must be lonely— but he wasn't. His boots still steamed and smelled of manure, and his cheek kept the scent of the cattle's flank. These things attended him unconsciously. The milk and the work and the morning—all were holy. Martin Bohlmann knew this.

At eighty-eight he doesn't talk much, nor did he ever. He gives his weight to a cane when he walks abroad these days. One of his eyes is blind, so it wanders sideways seeing nothing, or seeing invisible things. His hair is cantankerous, stubborn, unrepentant; his eyebrows are thick as briars; his nose is a plowshare; he is old, my father-in-law, and almost as mute with me as he was with his horses. But his spirit knows the holiness of God's creation, and though he doesn't say it, I can see it in that single sighted eye and in the step with which he walks a field: this farmer stands upon the earth with reverence.

Reverence: he gives honor to God who first gave earth to him, and him unto the earth, to keep it.

Reverence: that precisely is the stance I saw some twenty-one years ago when I found him alone on an early summer's eve in a field of seedling corn. He did not know I was there. He stood stock-still beneath a deepening amethyst sky, his hands inside the bib of his overalls, elbows folded like wings at his sides, his one-eyed gaze gone roaming over the corn to the far horizon. For thirty minutes I watched him watch the earth, in mute communion, until he grew into a solitary figure, black and motionless on the land. Humbly he loved what he was looking at. He, with the Lord and the soil, stood in a steadfast union. All was holy. And when I beheld this farmer's reverence, I knew the holiness too.

This summer past I've thought about my father-in-law. He and the farmers like him are my hope. They preserve in their very beings the truth that we, in sinful ignorance, have forgotten: that we belong to the earth, and the earth belongs to God. These are holy and living dependencies, as necessary as blood to flesh, as intimate as Martin Bohlmann and his horses. Surely I don't suppose that we shall live by the horse again; but I plead that we live on this earth with reverence.

Or what do we think it means that God gave us "dominion" over creation? That we possess it? That we can bend it to our own desires? That the earth is no more than a resource by which we support and satisfy ourselves? No! In the beginning, because we were created in God's image, our dominion was meant to image *God's* sovereignty over creation, *God's* personal and complete dominion, not our own. We were God's emblem within the universe, God's signature upon the work he had accomplished and then called "Good," God's stewards here below. We were placed here to serve God by serving the earth and so to be served by it. These are the intended relationships by the Lord of all. This is righteousness.

The earth is alive: thus Chief Seattle, Indian.

The living earth is holy: thus Martin Bohlmann, farmer.

And by his reverential stance the farmer calls again for honor to God and kindness to creation, that we dress and till and keep it rightly.

Look: we've shocked the earth by our colossal selfishness; and then when it fails in its rhythms, we are inconvenienced. But the farmer grieves. He looks at the heat and the drought as symptoms: a living, beloved thing is sickening.

Chief Seattle is dead.

Martin Bohlmann gazes across the fields that he kept for God for a while, and his single eye is sad.

12. Gaddy at Seventeen, Gaddy Again at Twenty

Why do you come to mind? Why do I think of you, Jimbo Gaddy, now—eighteen years since last I saw you?

I knew you, Jimbo.

I didn't know you at all.

You were a street kid, short for your seventeen years. You always came down to the center with slicked-back hair; but as the night wore on it loosened at the temples so that you took the appearance of a genial German watchmaker, callipers round your forehead. A false appearance. You could be lethal as flint. You were the spring wound tight inside the watch. I knew you.

Ice-blue eyes, an angular face, thin lips with a slight droop at the left corner. You smoked incessantly. The broad forehead encased a silent, running, angry brain. Jimbo, you played pool like a train on its track: you slid so lithely round the corners of the table, finding shots with a level gaze. You drew the poolstick back through the cradle of your fingers as slowly as crossing a trestle in Montana. But when that stick shot for the cue ball, it was a locomotive and mad: *Crack!* I thought the ivory would split in two. Instead it bulleted balls into pockets and, with a backspin, stopped dead on the velvet. But you hadn't varied your posture a whit, crouched at the table, your left arm bent, the cigarette curling smoke at your ice-blue eye. I knew you, Jimbo, shark. You seldom played for money. Cold, you acted as though you despised the game.

The things you seemed to despise were legion.

But you almost never spoke.

I ran a center for youth in those days, on Kingshighway in St. Louis. The people who lived around the center were second and third generation immigrants, come up from Ap-

palachia in the Depression, brought the Depression with
them, and kept it even to your day and mine. Poor. Your
family had never ascended from poverty.

This center was considered my ministry by those who employed me, who owned the basement hall in which we gathered; and at first I considered it a ministry too. I began with
a certain idealism, prepared to make a holy mark upon the
indigent, rapscallion youth, ready to model a better life in the
nights when the youth came down to play. But fairly quickly
idealism shattered against the faces of your people—and none
of you left me time or gave me the chance for ministry, at least
as I'd envisioned it. My work became a sort of policing action.

Well, on the very first night of my "ministry," six kids asked
for a van-ride home, and I felt gratified to be of service. But
five got out at the house they'd led me to, and the sixth, when
we were driving away, began to shriek with laughter. "Cathouse!" he screamed, beating himself about the head. "I can't
believe you was so easy. You took 'em to a cathouse!" I
learned suspicion.

The hall had a bowling alley at one end and a jukebox at the
other (playing "Hey, Jude" over and over till someone
reached in and cracked the record). Between these were Ping-
Pong tables, card tables, a soccer board, various civil games—
and dead center, the pool table. I opened at seven in the
evening. Immediately the lounging crowd came down. The
young ones came early, or else they'd get no time at the pool
table. The young ones strove to mimic their elders, and their
elders swaggered with rank impertinence. I learned to spot
members of the Tower Grove gang: they needn't swagger
quite so much. Their connections gave them rank and repute
wherever they went.

One sign that we were succeeding at something, according
to someone's standards, I suppose, was the swarm of children
perpetually at the doors of the hall. Thirteen was the cut-off
age. Teen was the ticket. But children thought something
significant was going on inside; so they would troop down the

outside steps and press their faces to the door. Sometimes men and full-fledged women appeared; but eighteen was the upper cut-off age—so I grew hard policing the place. I hated to see hip pockets thickened with bottles. But I grew hard and approached the offenders. Alcohol was forbidden. Pot was forbidden. Knives (if I could see them) were forbidden. "Take it out or get out yourself." And when people would not leave at closing time, I grew both harder and cunning. I developed a velvet voice and a winch of a hand for the smaller youth. For the beefier ones I pretended to call the cops. That cleared the hall. The youth were truly afraid of the cops.

But you, Jimbo. You moved through this circus separated, watching with an ice-blue eye.

And I knew you—jeans tight at the hip, your shirts forever pressed and buttoned at the cuff. I did. I knew, the instant before you did it, that you would jump me. I saw it coming.

There was a dance one Saturday night. There was a fee for entrance, and a girl at the door to take the fee. There was also the necessary rule: once in, stay in. Once out, you're out for the night. Simple.

Midway through the evening you arrived with your brother—a year older than you, more garrulous than you, but just as short. An argument developed at the door. I heard the shouting and came to check on the trouble. Your brother was pink-faced and furious with the girl taking fees.

The poor girl looked harassed.

She said, "They only paid one ticket."

Your brother stomped his foot at the outrage. "Paid for two!" he yelled. "There's two of us, we paid for two!"

You stood passively by, regarding me.

But there was no reason for the girl to lie, and the money she showed me was the price of one. I told your brother to pay or leave.

A quiet voice, a grammatical sentence, and a tone of absolute self-possession are sometimes strange among the poor, and can carry surprising force—the first time, and perhaps the second. Besides, I was bigger than your brother. He stomped and raged and left. And then there was you.

You said, "If my brother goes, so do I."

I said, "Once out, you're out for the night. You can't come back."

You dropped a cigarette to the floor and left.

When the dance was over, the girl was happy. "Made more money than we thought we would," she said. We began to clean the hall.

In a moment she came to me with a request. She said that you were at the door, that you wanted your money back again, since you hadn't come to the dance at all. She said we had enough to give you.

"Is he alone?" I said.

She said you were. So we agreed to mollify you and return the amount of one fee.

"Take Simon with you," I said, meaning her boyfriend, meaning: Be careful.

The girl and her boyfriend went out the door together and clumped up the outside steps. Even before the door swung shut I heard a yelp, and then a single, unbroken wail of fear. And I knew. And immediately I was running.

I burst through the door. I was bounding up the steps when I saw your brother fighting Simon on the ground. Where were you? Jimbo, suddenly I knew exactly where you were, exactly what you were doing. Still on the steps I whirled around and looked up. In that same instant you had jumped from the ledge above me. You were flying down with a knife in your hand.

Your weight knocked me backward to the sidewalk. You landed flat on my chest. But I had the advantage of foreknowledge and threw you off. So we rose and circled each other, you with a ridiculous serrated kitchen knife and an ice-blue eye. Then this is what I did: I drew an enormous breath, and I pointed my finger at you, and I bellowed, "I KNOW YOU, JIMBO GADDY! I KNOW YOU! GIVE ME THE KNIFE!"

Astonishingly, you did. And on that night, I was very confident that I did know you.

You neither answered nor revealed the least emotion. You gave me the knife, and you gazed at me.

I turned, then, and peeled your brother from poor Simon like the rind of a tangerine. Once you were out of it, your brother lost purpose and stature. He became a short, mad teenager. When I turned back to you, you had vanished.

So then I didn't see you for a while. Weeks, I think.

But I remember that you returned to the center one more time. Your hair was slicked, but your eyes were dilated and black, and I guessed that you were high on something. You slouched. You might have been smiling, but I said in my soul that you weren't. Jimbo, I didn't believe the smile.

And then there came a moment when we were leaning side by side against the pool table.

Suddenly you turned and hit me on the shoulder, a sharp, short knuckle-punch, which left a bruise. "Hey, man. Because!" you said right distinctly, and you nodded and you leered. I didn't think "smile." I thought "a thin-lipped leer."

"Because," you said again. "Because . . . we can rap, man, you and me. I like you because we rap!"

Rap. I promise you, Jimbo, that's the first time I had ever heard the word *rap*. I did not know what it meant.

Therefore, I said, "Yeah, we rap," and I hunched my shoulders and left you then, because I figured it for some sort of derision. And besides, you were leering. We never, never did rap after that. I never saw you again.

Rap. Now I know what it means. And now I know that I didn't know you at all. Once, in our relationship, you offered to talk with me. But I had grown hard and cunning and self-confident. I missed it. I didn't even recognize it. No, Jimbo Gaddy, ice-blue eyes, I didn't know you after all.

Rap. But I cannot hear that word today and not think of you. So I write you with half a notion that you might find this and read it eighteen years since last I saw you. And what I want to know is: How are you doing, Jimbo? Are you doing well, in spite of fools like me?

I wrote this piece for a newspaper a year ago. Jimbo never answered. Of course not.

Last month I happened to meet the man who had employed me at the center on Kingshighway. A happy accident. In the midst of our conversation, I said, "What about Jimbo Gaddy? Whatever happened to him?"

Paul said, "He died. Didn't you know?"

"Died?" I said. "Died?" The possibility had never occurred to me. "When?" I said.

"He was probably twenty when he died," said Paul. "A long time ago."

"But how?" I said.

"Oh, you know Jimbo," Paul said. "I think the cops were fed up with him. The word is they shot him when he walked into the pool hall."

13.   Emily Dichter, Surviving Past Ninety

I received by mail an invitation on pasteboard, signed with a flourish, to "lunch in her home with Mrs. Emily Dichter. Would you be so kind, sir?"

Sir? To whom could I be anything like *Sir?*

I knew the woman, of course. She attended the church where I assisted the pastor in ministry: an elderly lady, shaky on her walking stick, thick lenses in front of failing eyes, hunched down to tiny when she sat in a pew. She always came on the arm of her daughter, who was herself a woman in her sixties. The two of them lived together and alone. This much I knew.

What I didn't know was why she would invite me—or at the least, why she'd make such a to-do about it. If it was ministry she wanted, a phone call would have done as well. But in the whole year past she had never requested anything like ministry from me. I was responsible for education in the parish, for the youth, and for a host of minor duties, none of which involved her at all. Nor was I some luminary worthy of a formal lunch. I was young. A stripling. By day I did my job with competence in a large church full of luminaries. By night I gave myself backaches by bending over an Underwood typewriter, writing and rewriting stories with a sort of apologetic compulsion. Few people knew this obsession of mine. I would have been embarrassed for people to know it. No, nothing I could think of recommended me to Mrs. Emily Dichter.

Nevertheless, such an invitation felt like a summons.

Yes, I would be so kind. I accepted.

The woman did not live in the grandeur her card implied. But she lived in a valiant decorum.

Her daughter met me at the door of a four-room bungalow,

took my "wraps," and led me through a little "parlor" stuffed with books, into a little kitchen where Emily Dichter sat in state behind a little table. We shook hands (I bowing at the waist). Her daughter had to guide the old hand toward mine: Mrs. Dichter was nearly blind. But she pierced me! I swear, she pierced me with her milky, ancient eye. I sat. She never took her eyes from me.

This close, I could see how thin was her cloud of white hair. And age had simply broken her spine like a reed. She crouched of necessity.

She said, "Are you content, sir, in every particular?"

I assured her that I was.

"Then," she said, "before the repast, let me make my introductions." We might have been a royal party, but there were no more than three of us here; no more than three of us could fit in here. Emily Dichter was nearly ninety years old then. Until her last days she spoke that way: with a Jamesian rhetoric so florid it could shame a king.

"My daughter," she announced, "is my amanuensis. She has sight and reads for me. She has dexterity and writes my words on paper. You, sir, you are an author," she said, astonishing me, but never removing her eyes from my soul. She called me an author! She named my dream as though it were true. But she didn't even pause: "And myself I shall introduce in due time. Let us eat."

We ate. Rather, I ate; her daughter served; and the blind woman gazed at me, pleased, it seemed, by my appetite and my performance.

With dessert she said, "I've invited you here for three particular and valid reasons." She put her bird-claw hand on the knob of her stick, as though she would stand up to speak. She didn't stand; but I think she imagined a new posture for herself, one to accord with pronouncements.

"First," she said, "I am renewing old acquaintances. I knew your grandfather, sir, when he was pastor of our parish in Illinois. Fifty years ago and more. Mr. Dichter, my husband, served as principal of the day school of that parish. Your father was a boy. You yourself were not yet born.

"Second," she said, "as I have published a small book, I am an author like you. I wish you to know this regarding me. It is good for those of a common interest to recognize each other."

An author! This took my breath away. I did not know authors in those days, though I dearly desired to know them. Why had no one told me this about Emily Dichter before? Did she know what a dazzling gift to me her second reason was? The company of a published author! She must have known. She must have seen that I was grinning.

But her third reason, while it perplexed me with a mystery, outshone the second as the sun outshines the moon.

"Third," she said, still fixing me with her blind eye, still steadying herself on the knob of her stick, "I offer myself to you as a mentor, sir, if you wish it and will accept. Take time to decide. But an elder author can perhaps inure the younger to difficulties before they arise. I may perhaps walk you the rounds like a Virgil, sir." She smiled at her conceit. And then she leaned across the table and whispered with intensity, "But do accept. Never!" she whispered. "You should never, never be sentenced to dance in the dark!" She leaned back. "No one should. Not ever."

And so I was dismissed—not with a copy of her book. I was too shy to ask for it. She gave me instead a biography of Mozart and another of Chopin.

Of course I accepted her proposal. The woman had acknowledged me an author. What would I not accept from such generosity and insight?

I accepted her proposal, I say, but not with the veneration it deserved. I didn't know her story yet. But as we met more regularly, and as she disclosed herself the more and more to me, I learned that story, and I came to realize my extraordinary fortune. What she knew of writing, I was able quickly to equal. But what Emily Dichter knew of charity and sanctity and

sheer endurance, I shall never equal. Great church, we ought
to canonize such women for their outrageously loving spirits,
for their suffering (Mrs. Dichter suffered!), and for this: that
they could translate their pain not into vengeance but into
blessing.

I give you my Matron Saint, whose mentoring was my
epiphany.

Even from childhood Emily Dichter was compelled to write.
This was no choice for her. This was what she was. And while
she was young, in the last decade of the previous century,
people generally tolerated her curious hobby. They expected
adulthood and marriage to dispel her of fantasies, to school
her in duties and in her prescribed role.

Emily was no fool. She knew precisely what was expected of
her. This didn't mean, though, that she would cease what she
could not cease. Rather, she concealed it. And she continued
to write in privacy. After adulthood, no one read what she was
writing. (I marvel at this woman.)

And then she married. And then she had children to raise.
And her husband was Teacher Dichter, principal of the
school; therefore, she had a reputation to maintain. His reputation, her own interests being fiercely circumscribed by the
community, and by the church.

She did not not write. She could not *not* write. But she wrote
when the children were sleeping, in the afternoons when her
husband was working. She wrote behind drawn drapes where
no one would see her. She wrote in a perfect solitude—though
writing by its nature yearns a reader.

But this was the case in those days: that writing was fine for
students and essays and sermons and postcards; but *creative*
writing was a frivolity. And for women—conscientious
women, Christian and Lutheran women, pious women, the
wives of church officials—creative writing was considered
vainglorious, a vanity to be censured, a dereliction in wives

and mothers, a sin, and a sign of that womanish malady: hysteria.

I am not overstating the case. For though the church could be as civil as a Sunday suit, it knew exactly what it wanted of its people, and it knew how, piously, to shame the deviate.

Yet Emily Dichter wrote, and that's a boldness of spirit I can scarcely comprehend. She wrote. She must have been like Spanish Moss, surviving on air. She survived, though her identity was buried inside of her. She wrote, and what's more, she began helplessly, devoutly to write a book. An actual volume. Months and nights, and no one knew: this woman was birthing in longhand a biography of Katherine Luther. The wife of a teacher was honoring the wife of the fifteenth-century reformer. In utter solitude Emily Dichter produced a book.

And when the thing was done, she determined that this, at least, should have its reader. She wrapped the manuscript and laid it in a box and mailed it to the only publisher she knew, a Lutheran press. Then she put on her housewife's face and with burning nerves awaited reply from the publishing house—a terrible and thrilling time. In a very real sense, she might come to *be* by her book. I know such existential passions now. I am a writer like Emily.

The publisher answered.

Emily Dichter waited until she was alone. And then she took the letter into her dining room, slit the envelope, unfolded the single sheet of paper, and devoured three lines of print. "Congratulations. . . ."

"I was so delighted. Sir, I was so ecstatic," Emily Dichter said to me, "that I put my hands atop my head not to explode. I laughed aloud. I twirled me round the dining room like any child. My skirts ballooned, my arms went up, my hair flew backward, I cried for joy to God in heaven—and I danced. I danced. Oh, how I danced that day."

But before she danced her joy, Emily Dichter went to the window and shut the drapes.

The community must not see such vanity. The community

would despise the sin in her. Therefore, Emily Dichter, writer, splendor, God's bright eye—she danced in the dark. Alone.

This was the only book she ever published. Yet for the rest of her life she was an author!

Ninety years old, she said to me, "I offer myself as your mentor, sir." And she said, "You should never be sentenced to dance in the dark." Ninety! Emily Dichter, what you suffered, what you knew, and what you did with your knowledge! Woman!

She saw me. She pierced me to the core. Blind at ninety, that woman lived in a light of perception and mercy. She chose to preserve me from the sin that had buried her, to preserve me from the greater blindness of our heritage, the blunt insensitivity of our community, the prejudice and the oppression of our church. Is not this a wonder? She survived for fifty years on a single book. Identity bravely intact. In kindness, not in bitterness. Instead of vengeance or rage or despair, Emily Dichter chose to love and to bless. Yes, and I am blessed.

This is no less than epiphany. This is a miracle. This is a saint. Honor her!

Surely, great church, in the brightness of such saints we can see and confess our sins against women in the past, our demeaning of any who did not fit our easier categories, our dead-weight pressure upon lightsome spirits. Surely, in this sunlight, we shall not darken others hereafter. Surely we will recognize the personhood of each and each. In God's name, surely!

14. The Sign at the Center of Time

Hear another parable:

There was a woman who had two sons and no husband. It was her joy, her labor, and all her pain to raise her two sons on her own. They were bright and likely lads, of brown eyes and of black; and she loved them equally with a yearning love.

Before she left for work, she stroked their cheeks and gazed into their eyes. "Love each other," she said. When she returned from work, she cooked for them.

She watched in gratitude while her sons ate and enjoyed her food. She stole glances at them while they slept—her light-boned Brown, her Black so bold—and she wept.

Thus daily did she love them, but with a breaking heart and pain.

For they fought.

From the time they had learned to talk, her sons made weapons of their words and knives of their tongues; and fire both amber and jet would flash from their eyes. They hated each other. They said so, loud and heartily.

But their mother mothered both of them equally. She was the oneness and the blood between them. What else could make them one but she who bore them both?

Likewise, they together made up the whole of her heart. She loved them both as one. Therefore, their hatreds tore her heart in two, and she knew that things must change. She considered how this might be.

"I'll *teach them,*" she thought. "They have the skill of speech; surely they have the skill of hearing too. Surely a word from me will change them."

And so it was that in the evening, after supper, she spoke a wisdom to her sons.

"Blood should not quarrel," she said, "nor families fight. It's as simple as that and as lovely. This is goodness," she said, "that children should love each other as their mother loves them both. And if the example alone is not enough, if you cannot merely act like me, then take my love itself and give it to each other as though it were your own. Oh, my sons, I've twice too much for each of you. And if you share it, I'll have double that again. Why, I will swell with loving to see you love, and all will be nourished, and none endangered, no, not one!"

When this lesson was done, she took their faces between her hands and wept upon them with her tears, and behold: they wept as well with eyes both brown and black, because they loved their mother. They loved her truly.

But they did not love each other. And they did not stop their fighting.

They grew stout lads. They grew into sinewed youths, with muscles like traps and fists that could strike like serpents.

So now their fighting matured past taunts. It scorned mere words, it mastered the martial arts, and it flattered the lads as heroes, for they felt they had entered the real world now. Likewise, it cut their lips, and it split their knuckles, and it broke their noses too—all of which wrung the blood from their mother's heart.

It hurt her to see their broken faces, because she loved them. It hurt her to find their faces enraged, because she loved them. It hurt her still to find them divided, because they were together her fullness and all her heart. She knew that things must change. And seeing that words were nothing to them any more, she considered how this might be.

"I'll *show them* how much it hurts me," she thought, "and

then they'll stop. If not my words, my actions will change them surely."

So she waited for an opportunity; and as opportunities were daily now, this is what she did:

At dinner some minor insult produced a major offense, and straightway honor was involved. Looks became words between the lads, and words became deeds, and soon the combat was engaged, with great grabbings of ears and hair and noses, with punchings and bashings too.

Their mother did not speak. Instead she seized with two hands the hem of the tablecloth, all covered with dinner; and uttering a loud cry she pulled the linen backward.

Food and dishes crashed to the floor, and her sons were astonished: glasses and milk and meat and heartsblood spilled everywhere.

"You're killing me!" their mother screamed, her hands turned up in pleading. "The hate and the hurting are murdering me. Stop it, my Brown, my Black! Oh, stop it, please. Because I can't stop loving you—and love in me, as long as you hate, is a torment. It's a fire."

Then the two lads crept toward her and wept on her. They loved her. In that dramatic moment, they felt her pain.

But in the next moment each began to devise a method for turning shame to blame—for those who could talk, and could do, could also reason. And they kept on fighting, justified.

It's useless to number the reasons for their fighting. There are always reasons (though reasons are more often the pardoners of passion than the causes, and can therefore change with the weather). There are innumerable reasons, reasons on reserve, all of them indisputable, most of them asinine. Forget them. Hate's hate, however it is justified.

Know this alone: that the lads grew into men, and then they found more manly ways to prosecute their injuries and means more modern, more efficient, more technical, and less taxing of themselves.

They bought guns.

"O God!" their mother prayed. "What can I do to change them? To save them for me and from themselves?"

For here was a wonder: she loved them still, and her love was so rooted in her nature that she could not lose one of them and live. Yet she was losing both of them to their hatreds.

Thus she prayed, and thus she considered. And in the end she found a way, a terrible way. "I will *take their hate* upon myself," she whispered with an awful conviction, "and hope to take it away."

And so it happened.

Late on a certain Friday, late in a Lenten gloom, late in the life of a mother, when one son Brown spun round with his gun and shot at one son Black, it was found that their mother had come between them.

The bullet never reached his brother. Rather, like mortal hatred, it cut their mother crosswise and entered her heart, and she fell.

"Mama!" they shrieked. "Mama! Are you all right?"

"No," she murmured. "Not all right."

"Mama!" they wailed. "I didn't mean to hurt you."

"Yes, you did," she whispered. "You meant to hurt whoever was in your way. It was me, my sons. Till now you would not know. But it was always me."

And so she breathed her last. And she died.

Sons Brown and Black, what scalding tears they wept above the body of their mother! What lamentations they raised at this, her final act to save them good and whole and holy. Sorrow streamed down the faces she once had stroked, and they wailed like babies again, unable to think of tomorrow, unable to think, unable—

Which things, my blood kin, my family, are a parable. This is the middle of time and times, the half-time, this—and what are we going to do? It is time, now. What are we going to do? We, I say; for I am your brother Brown. And you—

15. Mary at Fourteen:
A Hug as Holy as the Ocean

Dear daughter Mary:

I snapped at you last week. I could justify my anger, I suppose, with good reasons, historically accurate reasons, could conclude our dispute with my own parental righteousness, and so be done.

But then I would miss your hug, and my forgiveness, and the face of Jesus in my daughter's face—and so would not be done at all. Self-righteousness is a miserly conclusion. Neither you nor I could come away the richer. And I cherish your hug. I love you, my fourteen-year-old, long-legged child.

My reasons for snapping at you? Well, I won't argue them. I'll simply set the scene with them. Even so, it's a whole battery of reasons I have:

We were forty people in the San Francisco airport. We were at the end of a California choir tour, going home to Indiana, tired. And I felt responsible for the lot of us. I was in no mood for anyone's negligence, least of all my daughter's.

By the time we gathered at gate seven we had already—all in a single morning—driven through thick traffic, had returned eight vans to Hertz, had checked over a hundred pieces of baggage, had lost Vicky Tyus's ticket, had spent an anxious half hour filing forms and buying her a new one, had searched the airport for wandering choir members, had begun to count heads at the gate—all, I say, before our noon departure. It is my nature to grow tense, even in easy circumstances. But Vicky's was the second ticket lost on that tour, the second ticket I had had to replace, and I was suffering visions of losing a human being to California. These were not easy circumstances. Tension in me had gone to torque. My smile was a plastic mask on my face.

Then, just minutes before boarding, there rose a hubbub down the concourse. I looked and saw the actor Danny Glover just as tense as me, signing autographs for thee.

I swam through people to retrieve you. But by the time I got there, Glover was gone and you, Mary, had vanished into the throng. But on the floor, like trash, lay your airplane ticket. Your life, sweet child! Your access home! And California was going to swallow you forever.

As a matter of fact, the choir tour from Los Angeles to San Francisco had been blessed in every respect, a genuinely Holy Week. This was the week of the Passion of our Lord. It was also a week of continual song, a week of unspeakable glory. Why should I have worried?

For we met the greater family of God and found it gracious. We had never been in Los Angeles before; yet when we came we weren't strangers.

Our very first concert, on Saturday night, was sung to a sea of faces black and brown and white. They looked exactly like us. Because you and I are white, Mary; but Lurena and Michelle are glossy black like panthers, and Dee Dee and Tim are in between. We're such a majority of minorities that we've got to be family wherever we go: The Sounds of Grace, over whom the dear old woman spread protection long ago. Remember? *Ain' no one stand in front of you for goodness, no. You the bes', babies. You the absolute best.* Often we've had to invoke that oracle in the past. Time and again we've had to affirm our worth by Odessa's words—whenever there were people who refused to be moved or to accept our singing, who fixed their faces like the white Alaskan tundra. But not that Saturday.

No, that heady mix of colors, that audience, received our singing right away. As soon as we sang of the suffering, they wept. When Dee Dee sang a solo of the sorrows of the past, they wept. When William sang to his own piano of death, they shook their heads and wept. And then, when we sang of the

Resurrection, they looked up and moaned, "Amen!" Their faces grew swiftly familiar to us, and when we chorused the excellence of the name of God, why, they put their palms together, and they clapped. They clapped and swayed with us. They made a thunder of joy. I grinned in such a generous company—and you, my Mary, smiled a dazzling smile. For I stood in front of you all, and I saw you.

We know what it's like to be rejected. We were not rejected here. Why should I have worried?

On Palm Sunday we worshiped with an omni-black congregation in Inglewood, shining obsidian they were; and we got back as good as we'd given the night before. God through us on Saturday was God *to* us on Sunday morning, a perfect circle. For the service lasted two hours long. "Lean back," it said from the start. "Relax. You're in for the duration." And the duration flamed with so genial a spirit that no one wished to be anywhere else. We sang to them. Then they sang to us. Then the preacher got up and preached to everyone. He preached with such intensity that a Baptist encouragement slipped from our lips. "Yes!" we whispered. "Preach it," we said. This was our brother, and he did. And when, in the middle of his sermon, he broke into outright song, Gloria Ferguson shot up beside me and whispered, "Oh!" with a strangled joy. "Oh!" she said, "the soles of my feet are tingling!"

On that particular morning our home was Inglewood, our house was this church building, and Jesus' was the blood that kinned us all. Amen, preacher! Amen and hallelujah!

What I'm trying to say, Mary, is that there was no good reason for me to worry about losing humans to California. God was in the people of that place. God was the God of those congregations, weaving us all together. So we were not foreigners. So how could anyone get lost?

And even when we were not among the people, God was there—God, with a majesty impossible to imagine.

After Los Angeles we drove north on the coastal highway

in rented vans, eight vehicles strung out in a balletic row. For two days the Pacific was on our left, and the hills were underneath us. Did you see it, Mary? And did you laugh for what you saw?

O Mary! The Lord has rimmed the sea in a slow white foam, like petticoats when seen from the cliffs above. And the cliffs themselves sweep down to the sea like stallions running. And the cliffs are robed in a crimson flower. And when we ourselves descended, we were overwhelmed by the heavy thunder of the breakers rolling. Black-brown and bulging was rock in the water. Waves rushed the rock, waves crashed the rock and threw to heaven white arms of jubilation—to heaven, immemorial blue. Then heaven and earth together proclaimed: *How excellent is thy name, O Lord! How excellent is thy name!*

No, God was never not nearby—

Nevertheless, at the end of this week of glory, you, my Mary, dropped your ticket on the airport floor—and I grew straightway angry.

So then: what has the power to cancel the vast community of Christ, to annihilate the granduer of the Creator in an instant? Great malevolence? Monstrous evil? No, petty irritations; minor fits of self-rightcousness; small exasperations. Mere faithlessness. I saw your ticket. I didn't see you. And all creation, and all the genial congregations in the world were suddenly nothing, and nothing was the passion of Jesus. I saw red. And I went looking for you.

And when I found you emerging from a public rest room, I snapped at you.

Then you put your head down, and you cried. Even now at fourteen, you cry so easily. Ah, my daughter, I'm sorry. I suppose I wiped out Holy Week for you as well. I'm sorry pettiness can be so deadly.

But listen to the grace of God: though sin may cancel the California coastline, yet forgiveness can restore it again. Forgiveness is nothing less than the regeneration of all the good that was and all that ought to be.

For on the plane, my gentle Mary, I sought you out, and I kneeled in the aisle beside your seat, and I told you my sin and my sorrow. How can I abide the tears of my daughter and do nothing? I whispered to your lowered head my confession. I gave you no reasons at all.

And then you, O child of God—you turned and hugged me. You put your arms around me; you laid your cheek to mine; and the ocean itself rushed back to me, and the week was holy again, for this precisely is the glory of that week, the immediate value of the passion.

God has given us nothing more practical and miraculous at once than forgiveness, nothing better for cleansing the sinner and curing his victim—no, nothing save Jesus, whose face I found in your face, beautiful Mary, whom I love with all my heart. You hugged me, and the cliffs rose noble all around me, and California Christendom declared, "Amen!" and I could scarcely breathe.

16. The Cicada

Exactly at eye level on the bark of the cherry tree in my backyard, I saw one cicada all alone. *Katy-bird?* I was seven years old that summer and happy. *Katy-bird, hello.*

She stood six legs tight to the tree-bark. She was the size of my mother's big toe, thick and blunt. An insect, surely—but I called her "bird" in my mind. Her face, aimed upward, looked like the front of a truck, the eyes set wide apart and separated by a sort of grillwork grimace. Her whole body was dull brown and hard as a husk.

But she had split her back from the neck to the butt, as it seemed to me. I mean, she had popped her skin like a pea pod and was slowly, slowly crawling from the shell of her old self. One cicada, but two cicadas, and the new cicada wasn't ugly at all, but soft and moist and sweetly green. Listen to me: a self emerging from itself. This was amazing. *REE-rrr-REE-rrr-REE-rrr:* the woodsaw song of enormous cicadas higher in the summer air. They were cheering her on, and so did I.

I watched while she struggled to climb from the hard brown husk, which kept the perfect image of herself, except that the face was empty now, its eye-windows like plastic bubbles clear and thoughtless. Her new face was attentive, sober. I gazed as she felt for a grip with her new front legs on the neck of old armor, and pulled. By degrees she dragged her green body through the crack in the casement. She rested. She twiddled her forelegs in fresh air. Then she pushed with the hinder legs, still inside. *Go! Go!* I helped her out with my desiring: *Be born, beautiful Katy-bird! Be!* Oh, what a summer's day!

And then she was standing fully on the back of her old form. Free! I felt very happy.

This was the end of a cycle seventeen years long, but I thought she had just been born today.

There were two crinkled packets on the back of the green
cicada. With her hindest legs she began, now, to tease these
packets, and then to brush them, as it were, and they opened.
They unwrinkled. Ah! I realized that they were wings, generous wings, each twice the length of her body. She brushed and
brushed. Sometimes she vibrated the wings at her shoulders,
as though she might try them out. But she had to stroke the
folds and creases from them first. This was a truly marvelous
thing to see—not the least because, when she spread them
out, these wings were—*Pretty,* I breathed in genuine gratitude.
Pretty, pretty wings! Ohhh!

There was a hair-fine network of green vein in each translu-
cent wing. It seemed that she was massaging blood into the
crepe of wing, in order to strengthen each toward flight. I was
transfixed. *Katy-bird:* she opened the soft wings to their full
imperial reach. *Pretty!* They stood like gossamer from her
body, the finest, sheerest glory. She began to vibrate them
with a purpose, now, preparing to fly—

But I was a child enchanted, seven years old. I had to touch.
I reached and touched one of her wings. As lightly as if it were
silk between my fingertips, I rubbed the wing. And then I was
astonished.

Green liquid spread in the tiniest rivulets within the mem-
brane. A pale green fluid broke from the threadlike vessels
and sank to the extremest tip of the wing, where it gathered;
and there it produced a single, lucent, sea-green drop—a perfect, solitary emerald. *Katy-bird!* I caught my breath, and then
I didn't breathe. I covered my mouth with two hands.

This was beautiful. This was utterly beautiful. I had never
seen such a beauty before, mute, inexplicable, its very own
reason for being, the center of everything: green, as deep as
heaven. The sun itself was in there, suspended as a point of
light. This jewel was so beautiful, that I felt a sort of soaring
in my soul. I wanted to laugh. *Katy-bird—*

But the cicada had not stopped vibrating her wings. The
purpose was to fly. I knew that. But now there was only one

wing that struck the air effectively. The other one, the wing
that I had touched, hung like a sack with its sea-green load.
Oh, no! Newborn things are terribly delicate. I said, *Katy-bird!*
Oh, no! I had hurt the wing. Now I began to breathe again. I
sucked a panicky breath. I couldn't undo the thing that I had
done. I said, *Katy-bird—I'm sorry!* Because the green liquid in
her wing—that was blood. That was her blood. She was bleed-
ing. The thing so beautiful to me was all her virtue and her
life. *Oh, Katy-bird!*

When she leaped from the back of her old shell, when she
reached into the air with one wing only, she dropped down to
the ground. On the hard dirt, then, she buzzed in circles on
one side, dragging a limp wing, which pointed to the center
of the circle. She would never, never fly.

I knelt down. I didn't feel like laughing any more. I wanted
to cry.

REE-rrr-REE-rrr-REE-rrr is the carpenter chorus of cicadas
in the summer—and still it seems to me that they sing an
unsearchable mystery, a song of astonished sorrow. For when
I wept above the dying cicada, I felt two moods intensely. I
couldn't abolish wonder at the beauty of that deep green
drop. Yet I cried to realize that to render such a beauty had
cost the life of a living thing. She spent everything she had.

And this is what I say today, when cicadas tear the air with
their incessant sawing: that God is making furniture. He's
cutting wood for a cradle and a cross. And Christ on the cross
is more beautiful than anything—for extreme is the cost of
extremest beauty. What I witnessed on that summer's day at
seven was the sign of sacrifice.

17. Matthew, Seven, Eight, and Nine

A Prologue to the Story of My Son

Twice in time God covenanted with humanity. Twice God sought to make a people his own and to keep them so. Twice the mighty God attempted relationship, both times with the clear intent that relationship should last forever.

Twice, I say, because the first time was a failure, but mercy found another way.

"You have seen what I did to the Egyptians," the Lord God said the first time, when it had come to its fulfillment: "and how I bore you on eagles' wings and brought you to myself." God had saved the people from their oppressors; had granted them, as a people, an identity; was shortly to give them a land, and wanted forever, for all time now, to maintain this relationship with them. So here, at Sinai, God uttered definitions of relationship with dramatic clarity and (it was hoped) unforgettable force: that the people's very identity depended upon their relationship with God; that the relationship with God depended upon their righteousness; that righteousness was their active obedience to the law of God. "Now therefore, if you will obey my voice," said the Lord God, "and keep my covenant, you shall be my own possession among all peoples; for all the earth is mine, and you shall be to me a kingdom of priests and a holy nation."

The first covenant was defined by a law and would continue so long as the law was faithfully obeyed. The benefits to the people were incalculable, life itself, and life with God. But God, not content that benefits would persuade them or that the people on their own could perceive the value of the benefits, walled the law around with threats on one side and promises on the other. Nothing was left to the imagination. God made the mountain tremble with his power, proof that he could certainly prosecute his intentions upon the earth. And then he said *If* over and over again, and he said *Do.* "Behold, I set before you this day a blessing and a curse: the blessing, if you obey the commandments of the Lord your God, which I command you this day, and the curse, if you do not obey the commandments of the Lord your God, but turn aside from the way which I command you this day." Thus, through his servant Moses. And the people said, "We will obey."

Again: "If you forsake the Lord and serve foreign gods, then he will turn and do you harm, and consume you, after having done you good." Thus, through his servant Joshua. And the people said, "Nay, but we will serve the Lord." Clearly, the covenant depended upon the people's obedience. Clearly, terrible things would happen if they did not obey. Clearly, the people knew this.

But again: "Seek the Lord and live! Seek good, and not evil, that you may live; and so the Lord, the God of hosts, will be with you. Hate evil, and love good, and establish justice in the gate; it may be that the Lord, the God of hosts, will be gracious to the remnant of Joseph." Thus, through his prophet Amos.

And likewise, through Hosea: "Return, O Israel, to the Lord your God, for you have stumbled because of your iniquity. They shall return and dwell beneath my shadow, they shall flourish as a garden."

Again and again the command went forth, with threat and with promise. And the reason it had to be repeated was this: it didn't work. The law, as definition of the covenant, could not maintain relationship. The people could not keep it.

Not for ignorance, obviously; for the people knew both the law and its consequence. Not for not trying; for the people repented often, and often attempted to renew obedience unto the Lord. When God made good on his threats, they tried. When their kingdoms fell, they tried. In exile, they tried. When God made good also on his promises, they tried. In the return from Babylon to Jerusalem, they tried. But generation to generation—in the slow progression through time—their essential nature always asserted itself, and then they failed. In time they always broke covenant with the Lord, because the imagination of human hearts is evil continually.

The law could frighten them; it could do that. The law could restrain them, that too. The law could blame them and shame them, estrange them from God. But the law could not change them. Mighty and threatful; clear, self-evident and logical; bountiful in recompense, the law might force people to *do* good things. But the law could not make them *good.* Their nature was obdurate to the law.

Therefore, the first covenant between God and humanity came to failure.

But mercy found another way.

God, who hitherto upheld but one side of the covenant, now chose to uphold both sides. If the people could not be righteous, then God would become their righteousness for them. Love no longer imposed love from above; but love came down, took flesh, became one with the people, and entered totally into the sorry sphere of human affairs. Love exposed love here below. God became, among the people, the very love that God had first required from the people. God, in Christ, fulfilled the second side of the covenant.

Mercy took a human face.

Jesus did not count equality with God a thing that he had to keep and never release. Though he had the power to make the mountains tremble, the authority to threaten and to bless, the divinity that can create or cancel universes, Jesus emptied himself and took the form of a servant. He became a human being, heir (though he was God) to all the weaknesses of human flesh, to pain and grieving, suffering and death. Obedient—as none before him ever was so perfectly obedient—he kept not only the good covenant of righteousness, but also the ruined covenant demanding death. He died. Was crucified, and died. Therefore, God exalted him above all others, that every other, seeing him, might worship; and any other might confess a faith in him, declaring, "Jesus Christ is Lord!" In that death and closure of the old covenant; in that exaltation before the face of all creation (that no one be neglected, but all have opportunity to see the new thing God has done); and in that confession of faith (these three) is a new and merciful covenant established. In Jesus' righteousness the unrighteous are granted, as a gift, relationship with God: a free gift. The law has been replaced by mercy! The second covenant works, because it no longer depends on the people, whose nature is iniquitous, but upon the Christ, whose nature is love purely.

Mercy took a human face.

And we have beheld its glory, glory as of the only Son from the Father. And from his fullness have we all received grace upon grace. For the law was given through Moses; grace and truth came through Jesus Christ!

But then here occurs a marvel that goes beyond the logic and theologies I've just recounted for you. Here is a marvel I did not know until I saw it in my son—but it is real, and Matthew is my evidence: *that we can be changed.*

Mercy has a human face. A human face can gaze at me, directly and personally. Then when I return the look, and when I discover a tear in Mercy's eye, and when suddenly I realize that that is *my* tear, *my* pain, suffered by Mercy itself and warmed by Mercy's love—then Mercy changes me. Sympathy disarms me. The willingness to take my pain (my worldly sorrow, my punishment, my sickness, my death) first to share it, but then to take it from me altogether, that is a killing sort of love: it destroys me. I can't comprehend its motive. My iniquitous nature is well able to understand the law: give to get. It feeds on the law. But mercy confounds me. Why would one, who doesn't have to hurt, hurt? Iniquity can't make sense of it; yet there it is, a tear in a human face! Argument fails me. My mouth is shut. My nature starves within me. It simply withers for want of substance in this new relationship. And mercy accomplishes what the law cannot: I am, in spite of myself, humbled. I die. And I am changed.

This is no longer the realm of theology. This is experience, spiritual and personal at once. It happens, and we change. This is consequence of an actual covenant: that mercy has a human face.

I learned it in the person of my second son, my Matthew.

The Story

I suppose I could account for his sins by speaking of his exuberance. From the beginning Matthew was an irrepressible child. Whims in him were deeds immediately. He didn't think. He acted. He wanted comic books. He took them.

Or perhaps I could explain his repeated stealing of comic books by pointing to his loyalties. Matthew was mildly hyperactive, single-minded in certain things, absolutely tenacious. He was *atropos,* the unturning, like fate. He stuck to his loves in spite of hindrances. These he overcame or ignored.

Or perhaps I could praise his astonishing self-awareness. Matthew was never muddled about Matthew. This brown bullet of a boy knew precisely the target of his attentions (adults should be so unconfused about desires and priorities); he knew exactly his own capacities, and therefore could be accurate: he shot himself, his whole self, forward to the predetermined mark again and again. Ever watchful, he never missed the sudden opportunity. When opportunities didn't appear, he made them up.

Whatever. Whatever meditations the boy's obsession forced me to, the fact has got to be spoken in plain, blunt syllables: *Matthew,* my second son, the child of his father's heart, *did,* from the age of seven, *steal comic books.*

And however I might account for it, I couldn't permit it. Stealing is wrong.

Therefore—given his exuberance, loyal ties, tenacity, and self-certitude—we engaged in a long drama, he and I: for I

would right my child! I mean, I had the responsibility of train-
ing him in righteousness. But though I had authority on my
side, and age and wisdom and the holy commandments of
God; though I was the one who taught the boy to walk and
took him in my arms and drew him with bands of love, the
more I called him, the more he went from me. Ah, my son!

Silly father! Goodness seems so plodding, lumpish, and
conventional next to a canny sin. What could I do to change
the soul of my son?

1. The Outlaw Exchange

Late one night (Matthew was in the second grade then; I was
an earnest pastor, earnest father, earnest generally in living
this complicated life) I heard soft bumping upstairs in his
bedroom. I climbed the stairs and saw soft light beneath his
door. I opened the door and saw my son himself, sitting on
the floor in underpants, surrounded by some threescore
comic books. The bottom drawer of his dresser stuck out like
an empty jaw. He grinned up at me. I blinked.

"Hi, Dad."

"Matthew, it's midnight."

The boy had thin legs in those days and a puff of Afro hair
around his face. "I know," he said. He said, with eyes wide
open: "I knooooow." Either he was enjoying an illicit thrill,
or else he was waiting for Dad's ax to fall. "I knooooow."

Was Dad supposed to have an ax, then? Was something
wronger in this room than a violated curfew?

Comic books.

"Matthew," I said, "where did you get all these comic
books?" Threescore comic books. More than half a hundred.
The kid was rich!

Honest (ever, ever honest!) he said, "The li-bary."

"You took them out," I said.

A light burst from his round brown face. Evidently, I'd hit
upon the exact right words. "I took them . . . out," he said.

That light made me suspicious. "You took them," I said, dropping the *out.*

"Yeah-ah-ah-ah," he said, light dimming, watching me.

"You're going to return them."

"Um," he said, as though that were another matter altogether, which required considering.

"Matthew!"

"Yeah, Dad?"

"You are going to return them."

He looked pained. "Yeah, Dad."

"Get in bed."

I'm not completely dense. I read books. I read children. My enterprising son had enriched himself with comic books he never intended to return. The operative word here is *steal.* He'd stolen them.

Steal, to me, is a witching word. It paralyzes my soul. It has the same resistless, spellbinding force as the word *lie.* When I was a child, my mother could use either word like a sorceress to fix me to the wall, for she despised these sins with all her heart, was horrified for the child who committed them, and was convinced that either sin would lead to the other sin, and both would drive her child to "perdition." *Did you steal? Don't lie to me!* So said my mother, and I was a maundering mess, immediately.

When I grew up and left home, these words lost something of their force. I put them away, I suppose, with the other frights of childhood, bogeymen and ghosts and so forth. Adulthood freed me, granted me a calmer perspective, more realistic, and less intense in moral matters. So I tended to view the peccadilloes of children with smiling toleration—

—until I became a father.

Until my own son showed signs of sinning.

Then suddenly the word *steal* returned to its primordial power. My son has *stolen* comic books! That plain scared me. What's more, my son did not seem overcome with guilt, neither for the act nor for my discovery of the act. The boy was as cool as a pagan. What then? Was he headed for perdition? The less scared he, the more scared me.

It was required that I do something. That I change the soul of my son, early, while it still was malleable. Matthew must learn the law.

And, by the grace of God, I had the means to teach him. I knew what I would do.

The East Branch Library sits right across the street from our house.

The librarian is a magnificent woman named Carolyn Outlaw.

Carolyn Outlaw stands tall and strong and staunch and absolutely moral. Her spine is not composed of bone, but of rectitude. Her eye can flash a holy lightning. Smoke and fire (it seems to me) do issue from her nostrils when she decrees the commands of God, the which she believes with conviction, the which she will impose on any child of any transgression. God is her God, and she is his prophet. More than a Moses, I would say that Carolyn Outlaw is Sinai itself, the Shekinah of the Almighty. And she, from the mountain, doth love the children.

Therefore, in order for Matthew to learn that the Law is not confined to our house only, but that it encompasses the world, that there is no place he can go apart from the Law, I decided to enlist the help of the librarian. On the following morning— earnestly—I entered East Branch Library.

"Carolyn," I said, "have you noticed an absence of books lately?"

"Well—" she said.

"Comic books?" I said.

"Yes!" she said. "All of them," she said, widening her eyes.

"We have a problem," I said. "A cunning kid, my Matthew."

"*All* of them?" she said.

"Carolyn," I said, "would you be willing to talk with the boy?"

Two tablets of stone doth Carolyn carry when she crosses

her arms. "Yes," she said, and my heart shrank for the sake of my son—for though I desired his change, I did most truly love the boy, and I feared the judgment I'd just prepared for him.

So then, that same day, father and son went forth from the front door of their house, in silence. The son was short, an innocent muff of Afro hair around his head, two eyes tremendously huge, like moons, just peeping over the top of two great stacks of comic books.

In a sort of a dirge march, father and son ascended the steps of the East Branch Library, massive steps, conceived like an altar by that distant figure, Andrew Carnegie.

Inside, the boy lifted his stacks of comic books and pushed them onto the counter—on the other side of which stood Sinaitic Carolyn Outlaw, regarding him with a reproving eye.

"Sir," said Carolyn Outlaw to me, not deigning to look at me, "excuse us, please."

I skulked from the library, leaving my son like Pipet alone in the presence of God and the Law.

Surely, surely, I thought as I paced on the sidewalk outside, the fire is worth the refinement. Surely, iniquity in my son will not be able to abide this Appearing. Surely, my Matthew will change.

The library door squeaked open. A little boy with an explosion of hair came creeping down the steps, his eyes as wide as Israel's. Side by side we went home again.

"Well, Matthew, did Mrs. Outlaw have something to say to you?"

He nodded.

"Did you understand what she said?"

He nodded.

"Did it have to do with . . . stealing?"

He nodded. I perceived that his poor eyes opened, like sunstroke, wider and wider.

"Will you ever . . . steal . . . again?"

He shook his head.

And I prayed, *Thank you, Jesus.*

2. The Fires

But the following summer I was contracted to teach for two weeks in St. Louis. I took the family with me. We lived in an apartment across the street from a park, around the corner from a drugstore. The park was free to my children the daylong through, while I taught. The drugstore was not.

But Matthew discovered the drugstore.

Several nights after we had returned home again, I went into my sons' bedroom, to pray with them and to put them to sleep.

"Jesus, Savior, wash away," we prayed, "all that has been wrong today. Help me every day to be, good and gentle, more like—"

In the middle of the prayer I noticed that the bottom drawer of Matthew's dresser sat halfway open. I would have nudged it closed with my foot—except that I saw the shine of a glossy paper within. I nudged it farther open.

"—Good and gentle," Matthew and Joseph were praying, "more like thee—"

I wasn't praying any more. My heart had sunk into my bowels. The bottom drawer was full of comic books. The comic books were smooth and new and many, many.

"—Good and gentle, more like thee," my Matthew was praying in sweet innocence. "Amen."

"Matthew."

"Yeah, Dad?"

"Where did you get these?"

The boy may have stolen. But he distinguished between sins in a manner that would have bewildered my mother's fierce system of ethics: he never lied.

"Fum," he said softly—taking thought, I suppose, as to how to phrase the answer. "Fum," he said with careful meditation, laying a finger to his cheek (while his brother was dying of an exquisite pain). "Fum," said Matthew without a sign of guilt, "St. Louis, Dad."

"They came home in the car with us, and I didn't see them?"

"Yeah," he said brightly, exulting, perhaps, in accomplishment.

"There is a reason why I didn't see them?"

"Yeah," he said more quietly.

This slow approach to the truth was wringing blood from Joseph's heart. *His* moral sensibilities suffered when his brother's did not.

"Matthew?"

"Yeah, Dad?"

"Where did you get these comic books?"

"Fum—" He returned to contemplations, true devotion showing in his face. "Fum—" he said.

Joseph, who couldn't stand it anymore, squeaked: "The drugstore!"

"Yeah," said Matthew, as though the thought had just occurred to him too. "The drugstore."

O God of our Fathers, and of our Mothers too—what was I going to do with my son? This was not a mistake any more or an isolated error. This, it seemed, was the character of the boy, the shape of his soul, and a foretaste of his future.

And I was a pastor who counseled other parents on the raising of their children. Was Joseph in pain for the sake of his brother? I was in anguish for the sake of my son—while Matthew seemed oblivious, cheerfully unregenerate. *The kid has done it again!* So what was I going to do about it now?

Their mother has always prayed that she would finally meet her children in heaven. My prayer has been a bit closer to the earth. I have always prayed that I would never meet them in jail.

What was I going to do to change my son, to make him good? I was frightened for him because suddenly jail did not seem so improbable. This time there could be no arguments of ignorance on his behalf: he did not *not* know. He knew; he did it anyway. A way of life!

Mighty Lord, my God and Judge, what was I—?

This is what I did: I took a leaf from my own mother's book. I invoked spectacular dramatics.

What I mean to say: my mother was a very poet of discipline. When she grew passionate, she spoke in the most colorful imagery. But my mother was a poet in the ancient sense of that word: if she *said* it, she felt compelled also to *do* it. Promises from the woman who despised lying—promises would surely be kept, even though they were uttered in the hyperbole of passion. Her discipline, then, was ever dramatic, always something of a spectacle.

When my brother could not decide how she should prepare his egg, he got his egg on the side of his head, raw and unprepared. She said she would, and therefore she did, wing it at him.

"Wash your mouth out with soap" was not a figure of speech with my mother.

And once when my brother and I were small, my mother said *If,* with a fine eye rolling: *If,* she said, *you do that again, I'll put you both in potato sacks!*

What the "that" was, I've long since forgotten. But whatever it was, we did it again. My avenging mother therefore bore down on us with gunny sacks in either hand. She did indeed bag us, stuffed us both in gunny sacks, then carried us, a boy beneath each arm, outside, to the alley, to the garbage cans in the alley—and she left us there.

So my brother and I rolled around in gunny sacks, conversing, enjoying ourselves (if the truth be told), because we'd never experienced the world from such a perspective before.

But then the neighbors began to gather and to cluck: *Mrs. Wangerin's put her children in the alley,* they said. Poor, conventional neighbors! *Why, she's left them for the garbage men!* they cried. They must have led narrow lives (so thought my brother and I)—no notion of what genuine excitement is. Excitement is living with a mother whose word is poetry, whose promise is her deed. *What's the matter with the woman?* fussed and blustered the neighbors. *Hey!* I shouted, fiercely loyal. *Hey!* I yelled from within my sack, ready to jump up and fight. *My mama knows what she's doing! I'm bad, all right? This is making me good. Go home and shut up!*

"Making me good."

For the sake of my son, then, I took a leaf from my mother's book of disciplines: let the lesson be dramatic! Let the child experience sin and sadness, all the spirits, the invisible world—that in the visible world he might be changed, be truly changed. Be changed, my son, my Matthew!

This is what I did:

I took him and all his comic books into the living room, where there was a fireplace. I placed him on the sofa, facing the fireplace. I kindled a roaring fire in the fireplace—then one by one, with slow inevitability, I consigned his comic books to the flames. *Whoom!* went the fire. *Whoom!* each time it swallowed a comic book. And I—in words as stern as Deuteronomy, words like rock for rhetoric, I preached. Threats and blessings. The Law.

I preached of the statutes and the covenant of God, *Whoom!* I focused on the seventh commandment in particular, *Whoom!* I veiled nothing, but spoke directly: Thou shalt not steal. There is right. And there is wrong. And the God who created the world loves the right and hates the wrong, *Whoom!* And those who do wrong also are wrong. Does the eight-year-old boy understand? The world will punish a thief. The world will reject the one who steals. But next to God, the world is nothing. Does the boy understand? Those whom God loves, God will take to Heaven. Those whom God rejects, well—*Whoom! Whoom!*

I never mentioned Hell. But I was determined to make the fireplace look like Hell. And I prayed that the small boy on the sofa got the idea. *WHOOM!*

Did Matthew understand?

He nodded slowly. He blinked and swallowed underneath his sinking Afro. He meant: he understood.

Oh, and I pleaded with God that he did. For his sake and for mine. Staging theophanies is dreadful labor—and I was the one who was sweating in the end.

3. The Punishment

But then this is what happened: in the next year my single-minded and tenacious son Matthew stole comic books again. A third time. He hadn't changed.

No matter any more how he did it. He did. No matter, either, how I discovered the repeated offense. I did. It matters only that it was me, and not he, who fell into despair at the act—for I loved my son. I loved him with a breaking heart. And I suffered dread at the thought of his future, truly, in this world and the next. How would I change the soul of my second son?

There were no choices left to me, nor other people to depend upon except myself, not Carolyn Outlaw, not the spirit of my mother. Myself.

I had to punish him.

I said, "Matthew."

"Yeah, Dad?"

"Go to my study. Wait for me. I'm going to spank you."

Wordlessly, he went. He closed the door. And then we both waited while in my head I planned the event ahead of me. Nothing should be done in anger, nothing in passion purely. But neither should I for pity foreshorten my arm and muddle the punishment. Oh, I was sad for what I had to do. This is the cold bite of a broken covenant. The curse.

So I went into my study, where Matthew sat small in the largest chair, his face both down and distant from me. The separation killed me. The child was mute in mystery. Then how could I reach his soul to change it?

I, too, sat. As clearly as I could, I repeated the law and the deed that broke the law. Did he understand?

He nodded. But then, he had always nodded.

Did he understand why I had to spank him?

He nodded.

So I called him to me, and he came. I laid him belly-down across my knees. These are the things I intended: to spank no part of him but his bottom; to use my bare hand in order to feel exactly what he felt; to swat five times, no more, no less. Five. Then pity wouldn't stall me, and anger wouldn't make the punishment unreasonable. Five.

I raised my hand.

The instant I brought it down upon his bottom, a hundred things converged in one. His muscles contracted in pain. He stiffened from skull to heel. I felt that pain. I mean, I felt more than my own sting: I felt the flow of *his* affliction. It ran from his flesh into my legs and hand. Like a fire it raced to my heart, and I groaned. Matthew didn't. Every one of his muscles tensed, but he made no sound. He shut his face. He did not cry. He refused. But I counted the requisite number of swats until they were done, three and four and five. Five.

Then I carried him back to his chair and set him down and told him that I would leave him alone a while, but that I would be back. Alone, I thought, because if he should cry he should do so in privacy, without the sense that I wanted to see his tears. Matthew, however, wasn't crying. I left the room.

And then I burst into tears.

Oh, this was more than I could stand. I bowed down and covered my face and sobbed.

Matthew's mother came to see what the matter was, but I could only hug her and lean on her and not speak. I was so sorry, so frightened and sorry.

Well, well. In a few moments I was quiet. I went to the kitchen and washed my face and returned to my study again. Discipline could not be over with the pain. Something better had to follow—and if I'd touched my son to hurt him, it seemed necessary to touch him again in kindness.

So I sat and recited again, all over again, the thing that had been wrong, the thing that should be right. And I said, "I love you. I love you, Matthew." I said, "I will never not love you, and I don't know if you will understand this, but it is my loving you that makes me do this thing to you." And then I got up and hugged him. Touch to hurt, oh, touch to heal again. I hugged him very, very hard.

4. The Second Covenant, the Truth

Everything I'm telling here is true.

And this is as true as any of it: that Matthew, my second son, was changed.

Never, never again did the boy steal comic books or any other thing—no, not another thing. That's categorical. That's a fact. For hadn't we gone a long, transfiguring drama in order to arrive at that fact? Yes, and once my son was accused of shoplifting, and I would have agreed with his accuser, except for the memory of that drama. His accuser was absolutely ignorant of the intimate matters of our household. But I had lived the drama through with Matthew. I, who had been the first to fear, who would have been the quickest to see a theft, I myself had become convinced of the marvelous change in Matthew. Therefore, perfectly trusting the goodness of my son, I confronted his accuser, and I spoke the truth. I said, "No. Matthew did not do the thing you think he did." I never wavered. I said, "Matthew does not steal."

What wasn't true, however, was how I thought the change had occurred in my son. I thought it was the spanking. I thought the law had done it.

The law can do many things, of course. It can frighten a child till his eyes go wide. It can restrain him and blame him and shame him, surely. But it cannot change him. So it was with Israel. So it is with all the people of God. So it was with Matthew. Mercy alone transfigures the human heart—mercy, which takes a human face.

For this is the final truth of my story:

Years after that spanking, Matthew and his mother were

driving home from the shopping center. They were discussing things that had happened in the past. The topic of comic books came up. They talked of how he used to steal them, and of how long the practice continued.

Matthew said, "But you know, Mom, I haven't stolen comic books for a long, long time."

His mother said, "I know." She drew the word out for gratitude: "I knoooow."

Matthew mused a moment, then said, "Do you know why I stopped the stealing?"

"Sure," said his mother. "Because Dad spanked you."

"No, Mom," said Matthew, my son, the child of my heart. He shook his head at his mother's mistake. "No," he said, "but because Dad *cried.*"

Hereafter, let every accuser of my son reckon with the mercy of God, and fall into a heap, and fail. For love accomplished what the law could not, and tears are more powerful than Sinai. Even the Prince of Accusers shall bring no charge against my son that the Final Judge shall not dismiss. Satan, you are defeated! My God has loved my Matthew.

Do you know why I stopped the stealing?

Sure. Because Dad spanked you.

No, Mom. No. But because Dad cried.

18.   Saxifrage, the Break-Rock

Once upon a time there was a child who did nothing but sit by her window and sigh. She believed that as long as she lived she could never open her mouth again. So she didn't.

Sometimes her daddy would slip into the room and tell her some interesting bit of business and then smile. But she wouldn't smile back at him. Maybe he would ask her a question about her day, but she wouldn't answer. She never opened her mouth. Someone might think that this was an arrogant girl, to be treating her father in such a manner; but the truth is that she loved her daddy, and it was exactly for love that she refused to open her mouth. She was afraid she might hurt him.

Of all the children in the world, she was the most beautiful. Her eyes were the haze at sunset. Her face was a loaf of bread come soft from the oven, smoky golden and so plump that it broke her daddy's heart to look at her—because of all the children in the world, she was the saddest too.

So he slipped from the room again in silence, sadly.

And the little girl would do what she always did, would stare through her window at the ragged streets of the city and sigh. There was a secret inside the child so dreadful that no one should ever discover it, a devil so dangerous no one should ever see. That's why she kept her mouth closed.

Now, it happened that a young man began to parade down the girl's street, right by her window.

"Melons!" he cried—but he pronounced it, "Mee-lohns!" and he was selling them. "Hey, great round mee-lohns for great round bellies! Mee-lohns sweet, for sweeter hearts!"

The little girl stared at him, but she gave him no expression, and perhaps he took that for a challenge. For he came back daily, every day. And every day he came back livelier than the day before.

"Whoop! I got me a load o' sweet fat corn! Green jackets an' yellow skin! Strip 'em bare, and bite right in!" He was always pushing a grocery cart full of goods, extolling his goods in shameless phrases—extolling himself, you know. A scam-man, folks might say. A jive salesman selling anything under the sun. A skinny whip of a hawker, tireless and happy, outrageously happy for these dreary streets.

"Greens all bitter to a black man's tongue!" he shouted, clapping his hands at his own fine rap. "Whoop! Greens to remember the hickory switches an' his ol' black mama, yeah!" The scam-man sent a distinct wink to the girl in the window, then roared on down the street, "Buy collard greens in honor of yo mamas, yeah!"

So one day it was melons, another corn, another greens. And then he came with fish he said he caught himself. And candles, crying, "I am the light!" And sometimes he gave it out that he was sharpening knives. And the scam-man danced in the middle of the street, and he shouted and sang and popped his lips and winked at the girl in the window. And inevitably, he drove his cart by a round route to the window itself, so that one day he snatched his hat from his head and made a low bow right in front of the child who watched him. He swooped his arm around himself like an actor of fame, peeped up at her, winked once more, then shuffled backward, butt-first, shaking with merriment, all full of himself, thoroughly impressed by his own theatrical ways.

The little girl stared. Who wouldn't? But she did not smile. She did not open her mouth. Yet something, when she saw that low bow, twitched deep inside of her. Perhaps it was gladness. Maybe just interest. It made her a tiny bit sorrier.

And so it went as the weeks went by:

The scam-man sang a signifying tune, strutting while he sang it, declaring his handsomeness (though he was bone-thin), his streetwise sass (though she never noticed that he made a sale), his inborn talents (though his tune was more raucous than melodious, more shout than song). He cut a ridiculous figure, tall and grand and skinny as a flagpole. And all this would have been fine with her, the daily diversion would have been pleasant to her, except that finally he did something terrible and wonderful at once, and the poor girl began to worry. Worse, she began to fear. The scam-man spoke directly *to her*.

"Hey, girl!" he cried suddenly, as though just noticing her. "Hey, you pretty pack o' somethin' in yo winda!" he shouted, sashaying toward her building, then stutter-stepping back again. He was shouting and dancing at once. "Why you never smile at me?" Oh, her tummy tightened then; he was talking to her, and he was talking about her. "Where you get the strength to fight my charms? Whoop! I'm a flat-down, jump-up strap of a beautiful boy, I am. The bes' o' the breed," he cried. "Then how you able to resist my irresistible style?"

He fired the questions at her, but he never waited for an answer, always twirling off as though stunned by the questions themselves, the marvelous mind in his own head.

The poor girl gazed at him. It was a low window; she was only slightly higher than his bony frame when he came close; but someone might have called her haughty anyway, as though she were watching from a high, embattled tower, because she never opened her mouth or smiled or broke her scowl or did any such thing.

" 'S okay! 'S okay!" the scam-man declared, most unperturbed. " 'S aw-right! One day I whittle you down, woody girl. But for today, I got m' things to sell, m' money to make, an' corporate business deals to transact. Bye, you pretty pack o' somethin'. Bye," he cried, "an' I be back!"

Then he and his cart and the show and the noise all clattered on down the street and away.

But the poor girl sat in her window and suffered. Things had changed. Because, for the first time since she shut her mouth forever, this outrageous fool had made her want to

laugh. *Flat-down, jump-up strap of a beautiful boy,* he had said, and
her stomach had squeezed with laughter. You can't control
your stomach. But you can fight it, and she did. By a mighty
act of will, the sad child had commanded the laugh to stay in
her stomach, where it became a dead lump of simple pain, and
the lump—it felt like sorrow. So now she wanted to cry. But
she didn't do that either.

She could not, and she would not, open her mouth for
anything, not for laughter, not for tears. If she so much as
smiled, her secret would show, and then even the happy salesman would be horrified by the evilness inside of her, and he
would run away with loathing, and that would be just one
more person whom she liked, but whom she killed.

So she kept her mouth shut soberly, and nothing in her face.
No, nothing at all, save sadness.

For this was the poor girl's secret: that she had no tongue
in her mouth as other people do. Instead, there was a snake.

Now, a snake in your mouth can be a shocking, frightfully
ugly thing. But it was worse than that. Snakes can also kill by
a bite of poison. And whom do they kill especially? The people
you love. So the only way to handle a snake is, keep it shut
behind your teeth. Never, never open your mouth, or the
snake will fly out and strike.

Twice the little girl had opened her mouth to people she
loved. Twice this serpent-tongue had struck. Twice it had
turned them to cold, cold stone. It should never happen again.
The child had learned her lesson. Never talk again.

So now you know why she sits so sadly in her window, and
now you know why she cannot laugh for the scam-man. She
is not haughty. She is dangerous.

For the first one that she turned to stone was her mother,
but then she wasn't sure that she had done it. She only had
suspicions.

But the second one that she turned to stone was her

brother, and that was the proof, because she saw the snake fly out. This is how it happened:

After their mother died (when the little girl still could not prove that it was her fault) she loved her brother more than ever. Their daddy was distant then. He worked the second shift, and when he was home he walked through the whole house groaning. So the little girl told her brother, "June, I will love you." And she thought of a way to say that they needed each other more than anything. She said, "June, I will love you just like mama."

And she did. She kept her word. She loved her brother desperately.

But after their mother died, the boy, who was ten years older than she, began to change. And they began to argue. And the more she loved him, the more they argued. So loving grew harder and harder inside of her.

In the evening she said, "Why you quit goin' to school, June?"

He was brushing and brushing his hair in front of a mirror. He stopped and said, "How you know that?"

She said, "Don' matter how, June. What matters is, where you get the lizard-skin shoes? Where you get your pleated pants?"

Nasty and uppity at once, he said, "Ain' none o' your business."

"*You* my business, June," she said. "You my brother. What you doin' in the daytime now? What you doin' in the night that shames you?"

"Shuddup," he said and went back to brushing his hair.

But she said, "Where you get your money now?"

And then he turned on her.

Her brother was always a wizard with words. He could make the language work for him, could talk himself into anything or out of anything. So now he aimed that language straight at her with no remorse, because he was changing.

"Licorice stick!" he called her, and she dropped her eyes,

and she felt the love go tight inside of her. "Domino!" he called her. "Peppercorn! Dirt! Charcoal brick—not a spark o' sense in your coal black head!" So she felt that the love was writhing inside of her. "Girl, you tar in a world that likes milk better, a sticky mess I step in," he snapped. "You slow me down, you hear?" Then he told her that he was wiping her from his shoe, and he strutted out the door, and he slammed it.

So the love got harder and harder inside of her. It felt like a thick thing in her throat, something she couldn't swallow. It felt like a rope that coiled in her breast, tight and terrible and evil, though she didn't understand how love could be evil. It made her tremble.

And then one night her brother came home, leering with liquor. She could smell it. He stood in her doorway and roused her up by shouting, and the dark was all around them. He was shouting about the worldly things he had done that night, things that she would never do, and therefore they were different, he said, so different. He was laughing nasty. And the more he laughed, the thicker grew the love in her throat. Huge: it blocked her breathing. Huge: it swelled like a vomit, and she thought that she was suffocating.

But then he said one thing too many, and suddenly, the love burst out on its own. She opened her mouth and she screamed at her brother. She screamed about the grief of their dead mama, and the bite in her scream was that she called him a vile, wicked, evil name, the worst she'd ever heard of—

No, sir! No, but she didn't scream at all. Something different happened, a monstrous, terrifying thing: the love that shot from her mouth, it was a snake, a long thick snake, a savage, hissing snake! It lunged from her stomach straight to her brother's face, and it bit him like hatred, though it was love—and she saw it! She gasped, and she sucked it back inside herself. Too late! Her brother was stunned. Her brother was frozen to absolute silence. Her brother stood in the doorway like stone. Stone!

Then neither she nor her brother talked. She was scared to

talk. He could not talk. The poison was in him. Cold and stony
went his face, paralyzed by the poison. Day to day he was a
walking statue, like the carving in the cemetery. It used to be
that the boy could talk himself out of anything. But two nights
later the police came and picked him off the street, like picking
a berry from a bush, and he said nothing to save himself, no,
nothing at all. So they put him in prison, then, as good as
dead.

And the poor girl knew that she had done it. Nobody but
her.

And now she had the proof, because she had seen it, and
she knew one other terrible thing as well. She was the one that
turned their mama into stone.

For their mama had been sick for many months, and the
little girl (she admitted it now) had grown tired of bringing her
mama water; the little girl (she remembered this clearly now)
had been mad that her mama was not getting up. In fact, the
little girl had let herself think that her mama should quit,
should be done with diseases and sicknesses and everything—
just quit and be done.

With all of these feelings inside of her, the little girl had
whispered in her mama's ear one night: "I love you, Mama.
I wished you would sleep the deepest sleep ever." Oh, poor,
sad, miserable girl! She got her wish.

On the following morning she had found her mother cold
in bed, all stony on the pillow, a dusty statue of herself.

And now that she had actually seen the snake that stunned
her brother, she knew what had happened. *I love you, Mama,*
was a little serpent that had snuck into her mama's ear, had
bitten a poison into her mama's brain, and her mama was
done with diseases now.

No one but the child had done this thing.

So now you know the reasons from beginning to end. Now
you know why the beautiful girl wore such a hard expression:
she was gritting her teeth against the serpent that curled in her
throat. She was saving the world, and especially those she

might love, from the snake. No laughing, no crying, no talking at all, because love in her was a danger to innocent people. The saddest, solemnest, soberest child in all the world: on account of love, she determined never to open her mouth again.

Yes, and all that is very well and good, and she might have succeeded in severity. But what about that skinny, signifying salesman who paraded past her window daily, daily, every day? Now, this was a complication truly in all her fierce determination! For you could frown like the Doom of God, but it didn't matter. The ridiculous fool kept coming anyway.

He varied the wares in his cart. He seemed to have infinite supplies. He bellowed his business all down the street, but eventually he wheeled his perfect self to the dark child, mute in her window.

And look what the scam-man came selling today: flowers. Potted plants.

And listen to his jive talk: boasts too outrageous to believe.

"This here," he declared, rummaging in his cart, "this here is magic for my stone sad girl!" He lifted a plant of purple-pink petals to the window ledge. He folded his hands and winked. "This here's the plant to pop you free, pretty girl," he announced. "Oh, yeah—*saxifrage!*" The name itself sent the fellow into a minor ecstasy. He grinned and clapped his hands and giggled with pleasure at himself. "Saxifrage!" he roared to the street. "Whew!" And he mopped his brow.

That little fit over, the scam-man applied his attention to the girl in her window. "Sacks o' what? my baby asks with the blinkin' of her eyes, on account o' she got a stone mouth and can't do nothin' but blink her eyes—"

The poor girl tried hard to cease all blinking of the eyes.

"Sacks, my baby wonders, of *what?*" repeated the scam-man. "Well, I tells her, don't I? Sax-i-*fridge,* says I, all full of my smartness. Pretty girl, this here's a plant of magical powers. It cracks the stones, they say, by touch alone. Able, they say, to cut what iron cannot bite—and they say truly. And maybe," the scam-man whispered in a low voice, "when I slip on down the street, you catch a notion to sniff the flowers. Maybe you put your lips to the petals. And then what? Whoop!" he shouted. "Then my magical plant crack open yo stony mouth. 'Cause that's what it does. It breaks rock. Whoop!"

He flew into a spiral dance over the wonderfulness of his plant.

In that same instant, the child snuck a peek at the delicate, pastel flowers—but the scam-man saw her interest and immediately slipped near to her. In a serious voice he murmured, "I know your affliction, girl. And you should know, it don't scare me none, no, not a bit—"

But straightway, even before she could lift her eyes, the skinny fool was back to dancing. His serious word had come and gone so swiftly that she wasn't sure he'd spoken at all.

"And how," he roared from the middle of the street, "do a plain street hawker come up with such a thing as saxifrage? Well, lemme tell you the story, girl." *Clap!* The scam-man made his dance an illustration of the story. He acted out the characters; and when he told of woodpeckers flying, why, he seemed himself to fly.

"Here's what he do, and here's what he already done: he track my brother woodpecker, whoop! to the woodpecker hole in a tree." *Clap!* "When the woodpecker flit away for food, the man, he climb and plug that hole." *Clap!* "My brother woodpecker, he come home to find his hole as hard's a rock, so the woodpecker fly away again for—saxifrage!" *Clap, clap, clap!* "What the woodpecker know by nature, the poor man can find out. Here come the woodpecker back, the pretty plant in his beak, you know. With saxifrage he crack that plug. With the magical plant, he break it! And when he don' need it no more, with that same sweet plant the smart man run away—to give it to his baby, oh me, oh my!" *Clap, clap—CLAP!*

The scam-man shot his shoulders to his ears, rolled his head left and right, and moaned in the deliciousness of himself. "Oh, baby, that man is *me,*" he fairly wept his pleasure. "And, baby, you—" he sang, now moving down the street with his cart and all his clangorous noise "—you cain't do no better than make a friend of me. I am so smart. I am so wonderful. A flat-down, jump-up strap of a beautiful boy, oh—"

And then he was gone.

There was only the plant on the window ledge, below her chin.

And the poor girl couldn't help herself. In the silence of the street, she started to cry. The tears rolled down her cheeks to drop on the purple-pink flowers, the sacks-of-something. But though she could not control the tears, she absolutely refused to open her mouth. She kept the ugliness, the writhing serpent, inside herself, imprisoned behind her teeth. Therefore, it was a miserable whimpering that she did, and not a true cry. Oh, how she wanted to love the laughing, signifying, jive-talking fool of a black-strap salesman. But loving him would horrify him. In her was the wicked power to kill him cold. So she kept her mouth closed and wept with a strange sound, like mewing.

Perhaps tears are the finest moisture for the saxifrage; for the delicate flower flourished. For every time the scam-man came by her now, the sad girl wept.

And he brought the silliest things for sale, things that had no meaning except for fictions and imagination.

Here he came with a jewelry box filigreed in silver, but nothing was in it that she could see. He held its bloodred velvet open to her gaze and whispered, "Treasures, girl, brighter than diamonds, better than pearls. Cain't see what's meant to be heard, though. It's names, my stone sad girl: one for you and one for me."

He closed the beautiful box and left, and she watered the plant on her window ledge with tears.

Then here he came with hollow lipstick tubes, laughing and slapping his skinny knee at the joke. He swore to her that this lipstick could paint pretty smiles on sorrowful lips—but only after saxifrage had broken the stone of his baby's mouth, he said. And he said it had three colors, one for happiness, one for joy, and one as red as jubilation.

And when he left, she poured a rich, warm water on the thirsty plant.

But then the scam-man performed a trick for which there was no joke, and the terrible love writhed so strongly in the poor girl that she couldn't stand it anymore.

For one day he stood by her window with nothing at all to sell but his good right hand, which he raised on high between them.

"Sad baby girl," he said, "it's free for the askin'. Let saxifrage just crack the thinnest line of a smile in your hard face, and this here splendid, sleek, magnificent prize of a perfect hand is yours. Oh, baby girl, it want to be yours. I axed it. It said, *Yeeeeah.*"

No smiling. Not the ghost of a smile. No words. No parting of her lips. But the tears streamed down her stony face like the rivers out of paradise, and love rose up like a cobra in her throat. She wanted to gasp.

But the scam-man took the forefinger of his good right hand and reached and touched her cheek and drew away one teardrop on the tip of his finger. And she gazed at this. He brought the teardrop down to himself and kissed it. Then she saw that her sorrow ran even to the corners of his lips. Love began to swell in her mouth, to press on the backs of her teeth. It was terrifying! She was losing control. Love was just about to split her determination and fly out—the lunging, killing serpent!

So with enormous grief, she pulled her head into her room, and she slammed her window shut against the scam-man and his plant, and she ran to an inside corner and crouched there and covered her mouth with both her hands, never to speak, never to cry, not even to sob—to be silent forever and ever. For she loved the scam-man now, and she didn't want to kill him.

Ah, pretty baby, more beautiful than all the children of the world, and sadder than any—ah!

So she sat in the corner, frightened and dazed.

Sometimes her daddy came in, but he sounded so woeful that she couldn't look at him.

"What can I do to help my daughter?" he pleaded.

But she didn't answer him, and he trudged from the room with lowly shoulders.

Scam-man, she thought, *do you see my window shut? Do you come? Do you look in this direction?*

And her daddy returned. "Once I had a wife, and my daughter had a mother," he groaned in the poor girl's hearing. "Once I had a son, and my daughter had a brother," he groaned. "Now I only have my daughter, and I'm losing her too."

But no matter what he said, she didn't answer him. She sat in the corner with her knees drawn up, and her arms around her knees, and her forehead down upon her kneecaps. And he left.

Scam-man, she thought, *what is your name? If ever I called you by your true name, what should I call you?*

And then one evening she heard a sound at her windowpane—a sharp, light, insistent sound, like pecking. *Tap-tap-tap.* And again, *Tap-tap-tap.* She raised her head and listened: *Tap-tap-tap.* But she wasn't going anywhere. Sadness had made her wise to all of the tricks of the world.

Then her daddy came in and squinted at the window. "What's that?" he said. "Well, ain't that strange," he said. "I never seen such a thing before. Hum. It's a woodpecker, come

knockin' at your winda. Hum." But her father had little interest for anything these days, and he left.

A woodpecker. Slowly, the sad small girl arose. Brother
woodpecker, *Tap-tap-tap.* Well, that wasn't dangerous. She
walked toward the window. *Tap-tap-tap.* The evening light was
grey. The room was shadows, and the window was a rectangle
of the dying light. *Tap-tap-tap:* she bent to peer at brother
woodpecker—but suddenly stood stiff and upright, shaking
with two almighty violent emotions.

It wasn't a woodpecker! It was the skinny scam-man, tap-
ping with his finger on the glass, come smiling as proud as you
please. And one of her feelings was the flood of love. Love
shot from her breast to the top of her head with such a tingling, she thought she would explode, and she almost cried,
You've come!

But the other feeling was terror—that she would cry a thing
at all.

No!

With his right hand the scam-man was pecking glass. In his
left hand he was holding the purple-pink blossom of the saxifrage. And with his eyes alone he murmured, *What I got for you,
m' baby girl—the bes' thing that there is. Peace.*

Then he touched the window with the blossom, and the
windowpanes melted and the wooden frame vanished like
smoke.

The poor girl shook and shook, for nothing divided them
now; but she could not move, and she would not scream.

No! No!

The scam-man continued to smile—a beautiful, soft, un-
troubled smile that had the mystery of killing in it—and at the
same time he continued to reach the saxifrage into her room,
closer and closer, until it brushed the poor girl's throat, and
she broke indeed. She plain exploded.

"Go away! Go away!" she screamed. "Get away from me—"

Then everything happened exactly as she knew it would.
Her words were not words at all. They were the venomous

serpent. The serpent sprang from her mouth and plunged
through the air. The scam-man threw up his right hand. The
serpent bit it in the palm, then flung its body like a single
muscle round the scam-man's neck and squeezed, and
squeezed. *Ah!* cried the child. There was suddenly a void in
her where the serpent had been lodging. *Ah!* she wailed, for
the serpent was strong and wrathful and wicked, and that was
herself; that was the length of her evil. *Ahhhhhh!* she shrieked,
no words at all, for she had no tongue.

The scam-man sank to his knees, strangled and looped at
his throat by the serpent. No one could tear that hideous
strength away. But the scam-man wasn't even trying. Instead
he was bending the serpent's head toward his mouth. With his
right hand, pierced by the fangs, he was setting the skull
between his teeth. He was biting it, biting till the skull-bones
cracked, and he crushed them. So the snake began to shudder.
It twisted belly-out and slid from the scam-man's shoulders
and fell.

But the poison was in the scam-man now, and everything,
everything happened exactly as the poor girl knew it would.

The scam-man looked at her once more in the dim light,
then sighed, then sat down on the walk, with his back to the
brick wall just below her window, and he bowed his head, and
quietly turned to stone. He died.

Scam-man?

He might have been black iron in the shape of a sitting man.
The moon arose to shine on the back of his skinny neck. He
might have been a statue, erected and then forgotten. But he
wasn't. He was the one who loved her, and she had done this
thing to him.

Scam-man? Can you hear me?

Ahhhhhhh! the poor girl wailed all inarticulate to the night.
Her mother, her brother, and now her friend. She made fists
and lifted them up to the sky—hateful, hateful child. The tears
streamed down the two sides of her face and splashed on the
leaves of the plant that once her love had given her. And he

had plucked the blossom, but he had left the green leaves here for her. *Ahhhhh,* she wailed. Her bitter tears were burning the leaves. They drooped. And they began to curl.

On the following morning, nothing arose. The sun did not arise. Instead, a dirty light, a guilty greylight crawled through the city, sucking the color from everything. The city streets stayed mostly empty. Maybe it was a Saturday. Maybe no one had work to do. The sky was a stony grey.

There was a girlchild sitting in her window, framed by the brick to look like the picture of desolation. She was a beautiful child, for her cheeks were rounded brown like muffins, and her face was the bread that is baked in an oven—but she was most painfully beautiful, because her eyes were sunken in sadness, her eyes were heavy and weary, as though she had not slept the whole night through. Her mouth was open. This was a curiosity, because it stayed that way: a coal black gap in the center of her face, a cave was her mouth—open, as though forever startled; open, as though the child were always just about to say a word; open, and perfectly empty. There were no words in there. Sometimes she said *Ahhhh,* and the tears rolled from her sad eyes down the muffin cheeks. But *Ahhhh* is not a word. It is a lamentation. And *Ahhhh* is all she said. Like the sun, this little girl did not arise that day.

Neither did the small herb plant on the window ledge below her chin. Not rising at all, the little leaves hung down in a mortal droop. They had yellowed. They had loosened their finger-hold on the stems of the plant, and every time the sad girl sighed, they trembled. And every time a small leaf caught a tear, it sank still farther down, as if the load were more than it could bear.

Under the girlchild, under the potted plant, under her window altogether and still and silent on the ground, lay a certain density, a stone—like all things else that dreary day, not arising.

Sometime during the day a man came into the room behind
the girl.

He said, "Is my ears lyin'?" He said, "Did I make it up? Or
is somebody makin' a sound in here?"

The sad girl drew a deep breath and said, *Ahhhh.*

"Honey?" said the man, almost panting for gladness.
"Honey, is that you? Is you talkin' now?"

Ahhhh, she said.

"Well, glory!" said the man. "Progress! You prized yo
mouth wide open! Oh, daughter, I could cry! Talk to me! Talk
to me! Say somethin' dear to me!"

But the child was weeping, and the only noise she made was
lamentation, and the big man behind her almost kneeled
down in pity.

Ahhhh, she said.

And he said, "Whatsa matter, honey? Please. I'll he'p you
the next step on yo way. What can I do for you?"

She was staring out her window; so he ran to the window
too, to see what she was seeing.

"Is that it?" he fairly shouted. "Is that what troubles my
daughter? Oh, honey, that ain't nothin'. I could clean the whole
street for you, if that'd perk my mis'able daughter up. But a
heap o' rock ain' nothin'. Girl, I'll get me a 'barrow or a truck or
somethin'. By tomorrow—you wait an' see. By tomorrow I'll
clear that heap o' rock from underneath your winda—"

"Ung!" cried the girl.

"I know, I know," said the man. "It's hard times, honey, but
it's a'most over now, an' I ain' goin' to let you suffer no
more—"

"Ung!" she cried.

"We got each other," he said. "Daddy an' daughter, we
unnerstand each other," he said, crushed by the weight of it
all. He sighed, and then he said, "Lemme go see if I can raise
a truck. By tomorrow, honey. I promise." He left.

Ahhhhhhhh! wailed the poor child, and all the dry leaves on
the small plant shivered.

But then for the rest of the day it seemed as if the girlchild were keeping watch. Her face grew stiff with determination. She folded her arms across her chest. She was a sentinel. She was a guard, like soldiers at the tomb. She never moved from the window.

So the grey light drained away. So the evening darkness sank on the city again. So a fitful breeze began to blow. And then two natural things occurred, both of them unremarkable in the order of the universe:

The little leaves of the plant on the window ledge, the dead leaves fell. The breeze had snapped them free, and now it hurried them down to the stone below. Like a soft crown they landed on the head of that stone; lightly they settled on its hands and its feet. Saxifrage nestled there.

And the other thing was this: a child lay down her head and fell asleep. She was too tired to watch forever.

The sun came up in the morning. First there was the bright light, and then there came a jangling, raucous sound from the distance down the street.

The little girl opened her eyes. Immediately she leaned out looked down for the scam-man, but he was gone. The walk below her window was empty. She jumped up. She was going to find her father and beat on his chest for anger, for taking the scam-man away in a truck. She was going to ask where he had taken him. But she only got as far as the doorway, because then she heard that jangling, raucous, unmusical, abrasive sound from down the street, and she stopped.

She heard: "Y'all think it's fish I'm sellin' today, but it ain't, hee-hee!"

She heard: "You suckers cock yo eye to m' wares, an' you say, 'Tain't fish.' An' you say, 'What is it? Eels?' An' you say, 'It's liver!' An' I say, No! Whoop! No! It's somethin' that all o' you need 'cause few o' you got it."

She heard: "Words! It's words! I'm sellin' words today!"

And then she heard: "Where's my baby at her winda? Where's that pretty face? Where's that chil' that never yet done tol' me her name? Where is she?"

So the little girl flew back to her window. *Scam-man?* Her poor heart swelled inside her chest. *Scam-man, is that you?* She stuck her head out into the street.

"Whoop! Whoop! There she be!"

And there was he—the prancing, dancing, spinning, cavorting scam-man, nudging his grocery cart on up the street, bowing to shuffle a few steps, then snapping his body upright and clapping for himself, his own best audience.

The little girl popped at the sight. Her brown cheeks cracked. She grabbed the top of her head with both hands and laughed through a mouth wide open, a liquid, wordless sort of laughter, like craziness.

Scam-man!

"Whoop!"

Oh, he was a beautiful piece of a dancer! Scam-man, black as the kick of a horse. Scam-man, skinny as a fishing pole, flicking left and right. Scam-man, limber and loose and light on his feet, not a notion of stone about him. The jabbering, jive-talking, signifying scam-man—alive!

"Whoop! Whoop!"

Oh, and that man was ugly. And how the little girl did love him!

Straight to her window he danced, and he thumped the ledge with his hand, like the perfect business deal had just been done. She laughed, delirious. He spun away and showed her his back, pumping his elbows for the sheer joy of being himself, bicycling his feet. "Oh, me, oh, my!" he moaned to the other side of the street. "I be style! I be beauty! I be my own self truly, oh!"

She laughed and laughed, clapping her hands and stretching her mouth with laughter.

"Saxifrage," he thundered, "do crack the hardest, deep-down damndest, coldest, deadest core of any rock! 'Cause, listen," he said, suddenly slipping back to the window and laying his hand on the little girl's cheek, "how my baby do laugh. Jus' listen to my baby now."

It was his good right hand.

In the nearness of the scam-man, the little girl fell suddenly quiet. She took his hand in hers and gazed at it. There was a wound there, but the wound had healed. She kissed the palm of his hand—and low and slow, the skinny man moaned, "Whoop." And she gazed into his smiling eyes, and he said, "Well, baby—whoop for sure."

Then he drew his hand away, and he said, "Pretty girl, I got some stuff in here." He rummaged through the grocery cart. He brought up a hollow lipstick tube. He screwed it open. Nothing there. Like an artist, he applied it to her lips and hummed at the wonder of what he was doing. "There," he murmured. "There, now. Her mouth is smilin', red as jubilation."

And it was. She felt the fire of smiling, ear to ear on her gladsome face.

He was rummaging in the grocery cart again, mumbling, " 'Tain't fish, nor liver neither, no. What I got here's the finest food I ever did serve." Then he brought up a strap of something that might have been rich toffee, for all she knew. But it was moist, and it shimmered in the morning light. It was supple, like silk.

"Baby, eat this," he said.

And she did. Cool and good, like a thickening cream it was. She swallowed it. Immediately she felt full. The great void inside of her was filled, even from her stomach to her mouth.

The scam-man narrowed his eye at her and whispered, "Baby, talk to me."

She gave him a curious look.

"Baby," he whispered, sharp-eyed, "talk to me. Say *Yes.*"

Soft and wonderful, as easy as breezes in the window frame, with perfect clarity and straight out loud, the little girl said: "Yes."

Her eyes flew open. The child was shocked by what she had done. The fire of smiling became a running conflagration. "Yes!" she gasped. "Yes, yes!" she shouted. "Scam-man! I said *Yes!*"

"An' that ain't all," he grinned right back at her. "What you got, baby girl, is a tongue in righteous condition. Ain' no kinks in that tongue, no—but words, yes, words an' truth an' chatter, yes! Speeches an' song an' a soft black rap, an' prayers an' beseechings an' praises, Amen, Alleluia! Yes! Ain' no end to the run o' language in that tongue, no. Oh, baby, baby!" The scam-man had begun to pant, was grinning, was overcome by the prodigy of himself. "Oh, baby, what I done give you—well, I cain't call it nothin' but a miracle, the firs' one ever, and the las' one too. What I done give you, pretty baby, is to talk like me! Whoop! *Whoop!*"

So then he had to go off and dance a while in the middle of the street, and she was trying to think of a song to sing as a rhythm for his dancing, since she could sing now, but for the first time she noticed a crown of the tiniest leaves encircling his brow, green leaves, dark and living leaves, but it seemed that they grew from the scam-man's flesh—

"Scam-man?" she called. "Scam-man? What's your—"

She was going to say *name,* but he threw up his hand and shouted, "One more thing! One more thing before your thing!" he cried. "An' sweeter than honey-wine this thing is too."

So he rummaged for the third time in his cart, and he brought up the jewelry box, all filigreed with silver; and grinning like a Christmas morning, he opened it below her gaze and showed her the bloodred velvet, upon which there was nothing. Oh, but it must have been the most precious nothing in the world, by the way in which he picked it up between two fingers, the rarest nothing that ever was. He raised it to her face and laid it lightly between her lips.

"Baby," he said, grinning like the melon split across its middle, "say it."

"Say what?" she said.

"What I give you," he said. "Baby, say your name."

The girlchild reached through the window and grabbed the scam-man's hands.

"My name?" she whispered.

He nodded. "I need for you to say your name."

Then, gazing into his eyes, she said, "Mary."

"Whoop," he said softly. "Mary."

She threw her arms around his skinny neck. She came fully out the window, and he embraced her too, with his own arms long as ropes, and she wept against the side of his face, "My name is Mary."

"An' now I can say," said the scam-man into this beautiful girlchild's ear, "what I been wantin' to say from the beginning of time. I love you, Mary. Mary, Mary, Mary, I love you. Whoop."

19. Three Liturgical Colors, And Time

Albus color inter omnes colores est prior purior, simplicior, et festivior.
And again: *Virdis color vividus est et visu jocundus atque comfortatus.*
—CLIFFORD, BISHOP OF LONDON, 1406

La couleur violette représente l'obscurité, las tristesse, et la pénitence.
—MALAIS

The first of the first day's dawn was white,
That detonation of Time—white;
That primal verb and the birth of being,
Fiat! from the yawp of God,
Was a shout of light,
Was a perfect howl of progenitive light—white!
   And in between,
    The whole earth springeth green.

Then this shall be the evening
End of Time's long westering—
When the phenomenal noun dispredicates
And the growl of God has closed debate
And the light descends in separates—
This: universal purple gloom.
   But in between,
    The whole earth springeth green.

And the Lord's intrusion in Time was white,
The re-murmuring of the First Word, white;
Then that advent requires a swaddling white.
But the King's conclusion's imperial;
For the Judge shall conjugate us all;
Oh, that advent demands a purple pall.
   Yet in between—
   All in between—
   The whole earth springeth green.

Wheat, and the young vine, green;
Shoots, and the small stalk, sweetly green;
And the tree unfolds and flattens high
A gang of hands to weave the sky,
An audience applauding light—
And green! Ten thousand leaves are busy green!
   For the grace of the spacious Time between
   Is the whole earth, springing green.
   All in between,
   The good earth springeth green.

THE FINAL ADVENT:
Purple

20. For, Behold, The Day Cometh

I had a dream. It was a simple dream, more feeling than detail, but it seemed to last a long while.

Simply, a friend of mine was coming to see me, and I was excited by the prospect. I didn't know who the friend was. That didn't seem odd. I suppose I didn't occupy myself with the question *Who.* Just with the anticipation, and with the certainty that he would come.

As the time for his arrival drew near and nearer, my excitement increased. I felt more and more like a child, beaming with my pleasure, distracted from all other pursuits, thinking of this one thing only. I found that laughter fell from me as easy as rain. I wanted to stand on the porch and bellow to the neighborhood, *My friend is coming!* Joy became a sort of swelling in my chest, and all my flesh began to tingle.

Well, it was clear that I hadn't seen this friend for years. Even in the intensity of excitement, I didn't picture him to myself. Perhaps I didn't know what he looked like. Is that possible? Yet I had no doubt that he was dear to me, and I to him; that he satisfied the fathomless need in me; and that it was me in particular whom he chose to visit. I could scarcely stand the waiting. Strangely, I think I expected to recognize him by his scent, by a certain smell I remembered, rich and steadfast, fleshly, warm, enveloping—like the strong declaration of a stallion's flank after galloping. It wasn't so much my eyes I strained, then, but my nostrils and the fullness of my mouth.

A wild kind of music attended my waiting. And the closer he came, the more exquisite grew this music—high violins rising higher by the sweetest, tightest, most piercing dissonance, reaching for, weeping for, the final resolve of his appearing.

And when the music had ascended to nearly impossible chords of wailing little notes; and when the familiar scent was a bounty around me; and when excitement had squeezed the breath from my lungs, I started to cry.

And he came.

Then I put my hands to my cheeks and cried and laughed at once.

He was looking directly at me, with mortal affection—and I grew so strong within his gaze. And I knew at once who he was. I was a perfect flame of the knowledge of his name. It was Jesus. He had come exactly as he said he would.

I cherish this dream and think of it often. I was a man full grown when I dreamt it.

On the other hand, when I was a child of ten or eleven years old, I was terrified by admonitions of the Judgment Day.

Generally it was late autumn or early winter when the pastor bethought himself to warn the world of flames and the falling stars, black suns and bloody moons, quakes, and the ruptures of tombs. Sin, it seemed, caused certain people to despair in the face of such disaster, and sin it was that caused the jaws of Hell to gape for them. *Jaws of Hell!* I saw those jaws, though the beast to which they were attached was too imposing even for my imagination; it filled the rest of creation, so far as I was concerned. And seeing that I harbored in me something very like despair in the face of such disasters, then I was a sinner— no doubt. Those jaws, with fangs like the columns in our church and drool like the rush of a flood, were open for me. The throat was backed by a purple curtain, a Byzantine reredos of marvelous complication, and a stone altar for a tongue. The throat of the Jaws of Hell looked exactly like the chancel of our church. I was destined to enter there. But by God, I was not, if I could help it, *going* to enter there. I had a plan.

Let me be historically accurate. In fact, our pastor was a kind and genial man, a bit grim when he taught us doctrine in confirmation class, but no more grim than any man with problems. He had a swarm of warts on his face; they might have affected his ease or unease with people, though one got used to the nodules and ceased to see them. Nevertheless, the pastor had them all burned off one day, so that he came back to confirmation class with brown pits instead of brown nodules, and we got used to them as well. He seemed somewhat tired when he taught us. He sighed more often than not. He had hair of a rough grain but a fine wave, lashes of a womanish length, and a stomach that announced itself even when covered by cassock, surplice, and stole.

The point is: of himself the pastor could not have generated the hard, ineluctable, dioramic images of the Day of Wrath. I think, honestly, that he had no notion of the horrors he produced in the mind of a child. No doubt, he meant the warning. And he believed implicitly in judgment. But what he whispered became a roar in me. What he barely touched (dutifully touched at that) became for me catastrophe. For the dreadfullest thing he did, the only-est thing he had to do, was to read from Holy Writ, in Jamesian rhythms all hoary with authority, the Signs of the End—and my teeth were unfixed and the roots of my hairs all tightened.

But when ye shall see the abomination of desolation, spoken of by Daniel the prophet, standing where it ought not, then let them that be in Judaea flee to the mountains.

What is "the abomination of desolation"? I had no idea. But these were words to conjure with. Their very sounds had Latinate potency, like locomotives. They would run you down if ever they got near.

For in those days shall be affliction, such as was not from the beginning of the creation which God created unto this time, neither shall be.

"Affliction" is a word I never heard, except under direst circumstance. A doctor used it once. And the superlative quality of this "affliction" was made fairly categorical: worse than anything since creation. That includes the flood. No, the pastor needed to add nothing to Scripture in order to terrify me. He need only read from Scripture:

But in those days, after that tribulation, the sun shall be darkened, and the moon shall not give her light. And the powers that are in heaven shall be shaken—and then shall they see the Son of man coming in the clouds with great power and glory.

Did you take careful note of those words? I did. The frightened child becomes a nearsighted rabbi for the words that frightened him, a scrutinizer of language, seeking escape. With a shock of joy I caught the words that no one else seemed ever to have noticed or to have glossed for us; words that formed the seed of my plan. These words: "Then shall they see."

And the words that followed were nearly as important:

And then shall he send his angels, and shall gather together his elect from the four winds, from the uttermost part of the earth to the uttermost part of heaven.

How many people do you suppose are encompassed between those two "uttermosts"? A thousand, would you say? A million? Billions and billions? A trillion? And when, in another portion of Scripture, it saith: "And before him shall be gathered all nations," how many more trillions of people does that add to the first trillion?

Ah! Now you have the two parts of my plan.

Part one: Early distant warning, "Then shall they see."

Part two: A mob.

I had it well worked out. During sermons—in the secret of my own mind—I made a hundred dry runs.

Before the Son of man transfigured this chancel into the yawning mouth of Hell, two jaws gaping for me particularly, *I would see him coming!*

Therefore, I always sat by a clear patch in our stained-glass windows, and I peered perpetually to the east. The instant I saw the corner of one cloud touch ground, whether shaped like a wheel or shaped like a throne or shaped like the prow of a boat, *bang!* I was going under the pew!

Then, while mighty footsteps of the Son of man gave lurch to the earth and shook the foundations of our own church, *whizz!* I would slip straight backward under six pews, break for the basement door, and shut myself in the boiler room.

Obviously, the Son of man shall concern himself with weightier, more majesterial matters than boiler rooms and boys—at least at the beginning of his manifest reign. He had kings to deal with, presidents, and schoolteachers. Now, I didn't fool myself into thinking that he would never get around to me. As great as my terror was for Hell, even so great must my sinship be. Such sinners the Lord would have listed somewhere.

But consider: millions, billions, trillions! Get it? By the time I peeped out from my dank hiding place, why, I'd be lost in the crowd. I wasn't coming out till I felt the rumble of nations outside, till I heard the myriad cacophony of seven foreign languages at least. I'd stretch the wait with sacred patience. But when I did come out, how much land do you suppose a trillion people covers? Shoulder to shoulder, I think they'd carpet the state of Texas, and not a blade of grass show through. Now, where do you think the Son of man is going to stand to see all those folks? Well, high up, is my guess. Very high up. I expect he'd be sitting somewhere near the sun. *Distant,* wouldn't you say? Olympian. Unapproachable. Exalted "on high."

No, he wasn't going to notice a boy of lightning reflexes and slippery strategies. No, he wouldn't miss one sinner. No: if I couldn't see his face in the uttermost remoteness of his glory, neither would he see mine. No, I was not going to be swallowed by the Jaws of Hell, whose tongue was a stone in the shape of a casket. Because I had a two-part plan. I was ready.

So, that's how it was when I was ten or eleven or twelve years old.

But then, when I was twelve or thirteen years old, all this came to pass, sort of. I mean, not point for point, of course, but in the essentials anyway. And I put my plan into effect. And I really believe it could have worked—except that the Jaws of Hell snapped quicker than I'd ever imagined, and subtler than I gave God credit for. What I mean to say is: the boiler room itself can be a Hell. Who would have guessed? The hiding place was a horrible place—though it *was* a hiding place indeed, and that's the part of the plan that worked. It's just that there comes a point when a boy simply can't abide the solitude any more, and then he's willing to take whatever's coming to him.

Well, and the Son of man turned out differently than I'd expected, too.

What do you think? Does the Son of man wear glasses? What do his eyebrows look like?

Let me begin this story at its beginning.

In those days my father was the President of Concordia Junior College, Edmonton, Alberta, Canada. One must capitalize that title throughout. It's a very high office that my father held. It holds an oaken authority, grim and altogether absolute.

Now, Concordia Junior College had a hockey rink in which, during the winter, students played hockey, but which, during the spring and summer, they abandoned. In the spring we faculty children claimed it for ourselves. We played football in its oval interior. The walls of the rink were a perfect border for privacy and for a football game; and the red and blue powder-paint had melted into the grass, leaving midfield and endfield stripes for play. The only problem with the field was stones. Winter always drove stones to the surface; and since we considered ourselves fleetest in stocking feet, we bruised ourselves on the occasional stone in the grass. But that was a problem soon mended. Every time we stepped on a stone, we tossed it over the wall, till none were left, and the summer was kind to the soles of our feet.

Now, I had my own method for tossing stones. I winged them toward one of the floodlights aloft on their poles, high and high above me. Because they were so distant, and I so indifferent a shot, I always missed the light bulbs. Winging and missing were traditional with me.

But there came the auburn afternoon when I winged a stone (and missed, of course), and a thrilling, stentorian man's voice called my name.

"Wally!"

My father, the President of the College, had happened to be walking by.

I stiffened, so to be seen, but I said with creditable innocence, "What?"—as though he had merely called, and I was merely answering.

"What are you doing?"

"Nothing."

"Wally!"

"What?"

"What are you doing?"

My father, willy-nilly, makes a juridical presentation of himself. He wore a black suit in those days, with a clerical collar white. His hair was nearly black, his glasses black-rimmed, and he twisted the ends of his eyebrows up, so they reached to his temples like raven's wings. His aspect was symmetrical, louvered, and sterner than he knew. Down the slope of those twin eyebrows came the gaze that turned his words to juggernauts. "What are you doing?" he said. How could I not respond?

"Winging," I said, "stones."

"At," he said, "six-thousand-watt light bulbs of great expense."

"But," I said—and I had a righteous defense—"I never hit them."

My father was not persuaded by righteousness or any rea-

son. "Don't!" he said. His raven eyebrows raised their wings.
"Don't you ever throw stones at light bulbs again." Thus the
commandment. My father departed.

But I knew better. I knew the undependability of my arm.
My father simply didn't understand the way of the world, or
of his son. I *always* missed. And besides: it was a tradition with
me.

Therefore, I continued to wing stones at the rink lights.

I suppose it was the last stone of the season. After that
stone, there would be clear running on a clear field, all heels
unbruised. I picked it up, drew back, and winged it, then stood
watching with my jaw wide open.

The instant it left my hand, I knew I had launched, for the
first time in my career, the perfect shot. It sailed upward on
a precise and beautiful trajectory. I should have been elated.
Just below the light bulb (which I saw with dreadful clarity) the
stone slowed and bent its path into an easy turn. But it closed
the distance. Its zenith *was* the light bulb, which it barely
touched as it passed underneath. That touch was enough, and
down with the stone came a rain of the finest glass, twinkling,
joyful, and nasty in the sunlight—

Don't ever throw stones again!

My poor heart sank.

My brother and my friends all gaped at me.

Don't you ever—

I thought I saw the cloud of judgment touching down to
earth, the wheel of the chariot, the prow of the ship—the black
shoe of my juridical father! I thought I saw him striding toward the rink, his raven's wings sweeping the sky with threat.
The President of the College, glorious authority, altogether
absolute.

But I had my plan, and *bang!* I went straight into hiding.
That is, I rounded on my brother and aimed a violent finger
at him and thundered, "Paul, don't you ever tell Dad." Then
I pointed at Feller and Randy and Dick and Jimmy Demos:

"Don't none of you ever breathe a word of this. Not ever, hear me? Not ever. Swear!"

They swore.

And so it was that I slipped into my boiler room, never, never to emerge until my father was busied by the multitudes, the masses of problems that all College Presidents must turn to one day and another.

I shut from my father a piece of me—forever.

It worked.

Or, let me be accurate: it worked for a while. He didn't know. He couldn't punish me.

But in time it began to seem that I'd shut more from my father than merely a piece of me; maybe it was the best piece; maybe it was most of me. Maybe, if he didn't know this piece of me, he didn't know me at all. I began to suffer the solitude.

Well, we would sit at the table for supper, and all my brothers and sisters would chat right openly with my father—but I couldn't. Not openly, at any rate. He'd ask some lightsome question, and I would reflect before I answered: what to answer, what not to answer. I would squirm, trying to remember little lies and strategies. He would give me a curious look, and I would know that he wasn't seeing all of me. Something of me was missing. So it felt as though most of me hadn't come to the table at all. My brothers and sisters had it so easy. I had it so hard.

And he used to call me an affectionate nickname in those days: "Ah-vee," he'd say, and chuck me on the shoulder, and maybe want to hug me. But I knew that I wasn't "Ah-vee" any more, that I didn't deserve the chuck—and that he would cease the affection immediately if he knew what sort of kid I really was. *Don't you ever!* But I did. *Six thousand watts!* Yes, and I broke it.

So when he said "Ah-vee," now, and smiled, it burned in my ear, and it shamed me crimson. I was growing so old so fast, so distant from my father, and he didn't know. He kept playing the old games. But "Ah-vee" wasn't here any more.

And one day my brother laughed at me. No discernible reason. He just laughed. But it sent me into a white fury, and I chased him. I thought he was laughing for his superior goodness—and he was right, and that made it worse. I thought he was laughing also for his secret knowledge of me—and I was angry. His very righteousness enraged me. So I punched him. I made a sharp knuckle of my middle finger and punched him on the bony part of his shoulder. He fell like a stone, straight down, clutching at his upper arm. And then he cursed me with the worst curse I'd ever heard; and the power of the curse was in its truth. He said, "Nobody likes you!" He said, "Don't you care that nobody likes you?" He disarmed me and broke me with that single curse. I saw the great hurt I'd given him, and the great evil that I had become, and I hated myself.

That evening, my father smiled at me where I lay on my bed. He said, "Ah-vee," and I burst into tears. His love scorched me, because it was a lie.

No, *I* was the lie. I'd fled to my boiler room. The room grew hotter than I could handle. I was so lonely, so desolated. I wanted to *be* "Ah-vee" again—but how could I be? My father was involved with the multitudes, the millions and trillions who presented themselves with honesty and humility, above ground, openly. They deserved his attentions. His eldest son deserved just nothing. Therefore, anything his father did for him intensified the worthlessness of his heart: *You liar! Look how you insult your father by making him play the fool!*

My father's love for me made him seem pitiful. But oh, what a wrath he would rise to, if he knew who I was truly! What a straking of the wind his raven's wings would leap to then!

So therefore I was caught between loneliness and corporal punishment, between the father whose love was a shame, and the father whose authority was Judgment Day. My dad or the President of Concordia Junior College: I had neither one.

Did I say I'd hidden in my boiler room? Well, now it felt

more like a torment. Now it was my Hell. And lo: the Jaws of Hell had not reached out to snatch me; rather, I'd simply walked into them. My plan had sent me in precisely the wrong direction, not from the weeping-and-gnashing-of-teeth, but to the solitary heart of it.

"Ah-vee."

"Dad, don't say that!"

"What? Why not?"

"Just—don't."

"Is my son growing up so fast? Is he a man now?"

"Just—don't."

And I burst into tears. I covered my head with my pillow and cried.

Paul was wrong. I *did* care that nobody liked me. Nobody knew me to like me.

So, then I couldn't stand my isolation any longer. So then, by main force and willpower, I determined to come out and to climb the mountain of God and to confront him with the truth. Then he could bundle me to Hell right properly. At least there would be honesty between us, and he would know whom he was sending to Hell. Then let the stars fall down. Let the high and distant Son of man sweep his hand across the sky to blacken the sun, to bloody the moon, to shake the earth, and to make the graves disgorge. At least I'd feel a deserving pain—a righteous pain, if you will—and in that sense would participate in one propriety. My stroke for justice. It seemed no little thing to me any more, even though I'd pay for it with my hide and the scorn of the Deity.

All of which is to say: I decided to go and tell my father what I'd done.

Strangely enough, his Judgment Day seemed easier to me than my own.

I came out of hiding.

Early morning on the next day, I crept from our house to the Administration Building of the College and entered its holiness.

I walked, with an echoing click of my heels, down long halls with high ceilings and dark oak woodwork. This building diminished me. *Authority,* it murmured all around me. *Sanctity. Probity. None of which are you.* My poor butt tingled and talked to me too: *You got us into this,* it said. *But I get the licking.* My butt felt big with anticipation, a heavy load behind me. I was apologetic, even to my butt.

And here was my father's office door. Huge. Oak. Dark. On a crosspiece of wood was affixed the legend: W. M. WANGERIN, PRESIDENT.

I tapped the door down low, little roach-kicks for a knock. "Come in."

Ah, me! There was life in there.

I turned the knob and nudged the door a little open. And a little farther open. And peeped in.

"Wally! What do you want?"

My father sat behind his desk, facing this door. A huge oak desk, it seemed to me. Dark wood. In the shape of a coffin.

My father's face was the focal center of the entire room. His black-rimmed glasses were circles of scrutiny, judging me, steady and unwinking, impartial and dire at once. He had brown eyes. He was twisting his left eyebrow between his thumb and forefinger, grooming the wing; for the raven of judgment was about to leap and fly before it stooped.

"Well?" he said, and I inched forward toward the desk.

"I," I said, laying a finger on the edge of oak wood, unable to look at him.

"You?"

"I . . . well—you know those six-thousand-watt light bulbs at the rink?"

"Yes?"

"Well, that's what I want to tell you." I waited, as if wanting *were* the telling.

"Yes?"

"Well. Yes. I broke one."

"Ah," said my father. "Did you climb a pole and bump it accidentally?"

"No."

"Ah. What then? What did you do?"

"I," I said, "threw a stone. . . ."

Slowly, my father arose behind his desk. I didn't look at him. Just as slowly, he rounded the far side and came toward me— black suit, black hair, black spectacles. Judgment cometh. The multitudes are gone. There are two of us after all. Only two.

I was prepared for the spanking. The order of things would be righted in my punishment. I lowered my head.

But I was altogether unprepared for what my father did. He broke me worse than my brother had done. I think I would not have cried if my father had spanked me. But he knelt down at my side, and he took me in his arms, and he hugged me, and then I began to cry, and I couldn't stop crying.

Love killed me. I hadn't expected love. I hadn't expected the most undeservéd thing, to be forgiven. That fire of my father's love—it melted me altogether, reduced me to a little mess, to a child again, for sure.

Oh, how pitifully I loved my father then! How God-like his love for me.

And he whispered, "Ah-vee, Ah-vee," and I didn't dispute his name for me; for I was, again, "Ah-vee."

So then, you see how that trashed my plan for shooting underneath the pews to the boiler room.

If my father forgave me the light bulb, what would my God not forgive me too? And if my father met me personally, between him and me alone, why should not my God be personal as well?

I haven't worked it all out yet. Likely, I will never work it out until it happens—since it will happen in a mystery. But I am persuaded of a paradox now. Somehow the King, who shall certainly hold court above the watching of a trillion people, shall also descend to me alone, shall find one child among the nations. High and glorious, and all people shall see him together: his dias will be magnificent—a mountain, maybe, or else the bloody moon. But at the same time he shall stand intimately in front of me. And he shall hug me.

Then why would I hide in boiler rooms, composing a Hell for myself? Why *wouldn't* I grow more and more excited at the prospect of his coming? For, almighty though he is, he shall arrive like the friend whom I haven't seen in ages. He shall mansion me with his good, strong stallion's scent. He shall meet me in music, a weeping adagio. He shall love me with his gazing eyes, and he shall dwell with me, and I shall be his child. And God himself shall wipe away all tears from my eyes; and there shall be no more death, neither sorrow, nor crying, neither shall there be any more pain. For the former things shall pass away. The mouth of the Lord hath spoken these things, and I have found them too in Holy Writ, for the Lord commanded John to write them.

In that day, the Lord shall make the whole world new.

When I grew to be an adult, I dreamed that I met Jesus. A lovely dream, but it was just a dream.

The advent itself is ahead of me still, and that shall be no dream. It is a promise now; it will be the single most overwhelming event in the universe when it occurs. I confess that I tremble at the thought of the coming of One who shall dispopulate the graves and assemble the peoples and transfigure the whole of creation. But it is the grandeur, the uttermost awe of the thing that causes me to tremble. I am not afraid. And I will not hide. I wait in a purple contemplation, peering through a clear patch in the stained-glass window. I watch, and I wait.

21. The Signs of the Times

"Ye can discern the face of the sky; but can ye not discern the signs of the times?"

I.

Mystacoceti! The whale displaces ocean where she goes;
The blue whale sweeps the sea, piling the element before
   her,
Drawing long green lines like ribbons down her body,
Lines of the crushing of sunlight, the rimming of
   marine-light, green,
Lines latitudinal (she bends the Capricorn to make her
   passage),
Water-lines that swoop her face and close behind her
   flukes. . . .

And can the krill not know what bulk approaches?
Does no fore-shock warn their myriad rocking economies,
No radiating wave, no surge precede,
Impacting them then sucking them apart in liquid rhythm,
Causing them a cold excitement at the advent?
God is coming! God is coming!
All the element we swim in, this existence,
Echoes ahead the advent. God is coming! Can't you feel it?

II.

If sound is color,
Brown surrounds the cougar.

He thickens the atmosphere,
Hushing it.

This predator prowls forever
A studious depression of light—
All the small deer falling silent,
Dimming their mammal-lights at his approach
To study survival
Privately,
To contemplate his eye with wide ears
Solemnly;
They cowl their boisterous lives in brown—
And the cougar is the vortex of a forest silence.

Only the fool,
When the brown cloud, Quiet, overshadows him,
Stilling the grasses even at his chin,
Does not know the cougar causes the weather.
Unschooled, the damn fool laughs
And is eaten.

God is coming.
Have you no ears? No fears?
No eyes to see the silencing?
Look to the muting of the spheres.
Listen to the tarnish of the skies.
Why, the wind itself is tawny,
Contracting toward a lunge—
God is coming,
And not one canny mammal,
Mother of a small brood,
Moves.

III.

In the days of the angels—
The hair on the necks of the people,
Didn't it stand like static?

In the days of the angels—
The air at their ears, the cloud in the heavens,
Didn't it crack like a solid?

In the days when the angels dropped,
   Discharging news in the troposphere—
Could such electric language not
Have shot the nerves of the firmament
With signs, signs?
White words and understanding?

Skin,
The abdomen,
And deep the human womb,
Must have been
Tympanic then.

Ho! In the days when archangels spoke—
Wasn't the smell of the weather ozone
Tasting of seltzer and ions?
And the look of the air thereafter—
Wasn't it crystalline, cleaner,
Dimensioned by nitrogen oxides,
As somebody's breathing
Swells with well-being?
Wasn't the breeze of the evening green?

Surely the people perceived
That angels were immanent, speaking:

   "*A son*—"
Now, there's a bolt to strike an old man dumb.
One hundred bidders in the courtyard,
Jews devout at the hour of incense,
Should have been shocked in their nostrils,
Charged by a nitrogous excitement,
Their blood in a rush of bubbles.

   "*A Son*—"
Let a maiden grab her skirts and run.
Let citizens stare after her,
Stunned, wondering
Why Modesty goes forking through the streets,
Her knees indecently aflame,
Her hair unpinned, a fume on the wind:
"Cousin! Cousin! I've such a thing to tell you!"

   "*A virgin's Son*—"
And the father who hadn't engendered it
Sprang from his pillow,
The crack of prophecy still ringing in his ears.
Surely Nazareth was startled with him,
Surely Galilee!
Surely Rome
At such an impossible pop of lightning
Moaned in her sleep.

"*A Savior!*"
Then all the stars, the wheeling galaxy, streamed down
Exploding songs of fire across the firmament,
Sheeting the fields of shepherds in a flaming rain,
Gloria, roaring: *Gloria in altissimis Deo,*
The storm of heaven striking earth,
All angels in a fusillade!
Could anyone, could anyone have stayed asleep
When the whole air burned electric blue
And every hair on every head was singed?

Well, if they did
They smelled the smoke in the morning
And didn't understand
It was themselves
Whom God had scorched.

But the leaves grew greener in their season.
The vines were nourished by the nitrogen.
Oh, grapevines comprehend an angel's discharge—
And vineyards that year produced a wine so red
That fools who lifted glasses to the sun
Were made uneasy by the crimson lens
And the dim suspicion
They were drinking blood.

IV.

But the salmon
  Shooting from a shattered water
  Knows;

And the falcon knows
  On her shelf of wind
  The instant before she stoops;

And the doe who suddenly
  Lifts her face from a bank of fern
  Twisting her ears like dishes,

And the prairie dogs
  All standing watch on the tableland
  Erect as pepper shakers,

And the ant
  Twiddling her feelers in the universe,

And the rabbit
  Caught in the gloaming of the cougar,

And the krill
  Upheaving on an advent of oceanwater—

All these,
  At the terminal nerves of their beings,
  Know *Kairos,*
  The fullness of time,
  That the storm of the Lord is at hand.

They long for the crack of liberty
  Of all creation,
  Groaning an intensity
  Of waitfulness.

They have unsullied senses:
 Watch them. Call them kin.

Oh, ye nations!
 Let these be your angels!

22.   Telling Time

A tree fell down in Bayard Park last Sunday. There was no warning.

Near seven in the evening the floor and the foundation of our house shook, just once, suddenly, like a spasm; the walls made a sound of dull booming; then there followed an awful hush. When the whole house shakes, it's as if the universe did, and for a moment I couldn't guess the source of the jolt. I sat waiting for another. I remember that I held a coffee cup at my lips.

But the silence extended itself—and then it resolved into birdsong outside, and the dog began to bark.

So I went to the back window where the dog was, and I looked and I saw that the world had changed.

Not thirty feet from our fence a massive, grizzled, many-branched tree had laid himself upon the ground and died. Him whom I had scarcely noticed standing, I marveled at now down. So broad had been his reach before, that now the lateral branches fountained higher than the young trees beside him. He was oak. At prime the dogwood would never grow as tall as the oak in death.

But dogwood and rosebud and the flowering locust were all who stood attendance on the old oak in the first moments after his fall (except that the dog was going crazy with his barking). No people yet. No one had cut him down. No storm had hit him. The weather was perfectly calm. Neither the wind nor humankind had engineered this end; but he must have felt an eschaton in his inward parts; and despite an outward show of luxuriance and strength, he had obeyed, had split his trunk and fallen down. Oh, but he was huge in death! He seemed a solitary entity. All by himself he caused a forest in the park. I confess, I looked at him with awe.

But the dog kept straining the leash and barking, and it dawned on me that a child might be pinned beneath the tree. I shot outside, crossed to the park, and circled the tree, feeling a bit of fear. I pulled the foliage aside and peered within. Some of the sturdier limbs had cracked and plunged into the earth. There were green caverns in the tree's embrace—but there were no children there. So the fear passed away and simple awe remained. The corpse was enormous, and it seemed something of a privilege that I could come so near to what had been exalted and unreachable before, that I could touch the topmost branches, could gaze into the interior and see the Titan's skeleton.

Neighbors began to gather then, gazing too and scratching their chins.

"Well, well, well."

I was glad that they came. I thought that with the dogwood and the rosebud we were sharing wonder.

"Big ol' tree, ain't it!"

"Oak."

"Hunnert an' thirty feet, if it's a foot!"

"White oak, I'd say."

"I *told* the Park's Department this would happen! 'Dag-gone,' I told them. I said 'we got us a hazard here.' But do you think they'd even come to look at it?"

"No, no—*red* oak. It's the red oak grows taller than the white."

"What'd you expect? They ain't been out to mow the grass. You think they'll check a tree?"

"Mm-mm! Hunnert an' thirty feet! What's that in board-feet?"

"Firewood, brother!"

"So what's that in cords?"

"Lucky thing it fell that way and not this. Coulda taken out the Wangerin house."

"Nope! It's the white oak that's got this-sheer grey colored bark. This-sheer's a white oak tree."

"Shoot! This is ridic'lous. I'm goin' in to call the Park's Department right now!"

"Closed on Sunday."

"That don' matter to me! I'm mad!"

So spoke the neighbors among themselves while the sun descended, and I grew somewhat lonely. Did no one else think this a solemn moment? Was I foolish to feel stirred by the fall of a colossal tree? Shouldn't we be whispering? This ancient had, after all, lived a life longer than any of ours, longer, in fact, than the history of this city.

But, "Good firewood, once it's cured," the neighbors said, and they began to depart in the darkness.

On Monday the children came. They made delighted noises outside my window. They made of the fallen tree a world, his horizontal trunk a highway, his branches their dens and hiding places. There must have been a score of children scooting through the maze, calling to one another, laughing, scrapping, and chirruping. They looked like fat, colorful birds, busy about their lives in the greenwood—and I agreed with their decision. Their instincts seemed perfectly right to me: the tree was a cosmos, many-leveled. His name was Yggdrasil.

On Tuesday the Park's Department appeared in cold green trucks. It is forbidden to drive vehicles into the park—but these are those who make the laws in the first place. They crossed the lawn and surrounded Yggdrasil with trucks. Chain saws spluttered in the morning air, then rose to a regular nasal snarl and got down to work. They whined into the wood. They severed the branches, lopped and sectioned the greater limbs, brought the high leaves, trembling, downward as though they were flags whose poles had been chopped. They scattered twigs and leaves and bits of bark all over the ground, a sort of a dry gore. They spat sawdust wherever they chewed. Tuesday and Wednesday the cutting continued, and children were nowhere in sight. My dog grew tired of barking. The chainsaws girdled the ancient trunk. In the end, like a spine divided into vertebrae, they left it broken in pieces.

On Thursday and Friday the neighbors returned with station wagons and pick-up trucks. Scavangers now, they selected logs and small wood for their fireplaces. Some of the more ambitious chopped what they couldn't lift, chopped long into the night, with axes and wedges reducing the bigger timber to burnable sizes, to load their wood-stoves with. I lay in bed and listened to the tireless *chop, chop, chop.*

This is Saturday, the sixth day. The tree is gone now: his hugeness, his shape, his long history, his hoary dignity all gone without a monument—except that the largest wheel of his trunk still lies unburied. He is his own memorial. The ruptured stump is standing.

And I'm a little sad.

It seems to me that nothing should pass without some recognition and reverence, some awe-ful reading of the legend written before us. Every passing betokens Time's Passing.

My city is utilitarian. My neighbors are realists, a good and practical people. But we are a nation without a myth. We have no means to read the signs and by the signs to see the truth.

Even the dog knows when to bark.

But we will say, "There's no such thing as a Yggdrasil," and go on about our daily business, turning a tree into firewood, ignorant totally of how close we have come to the Twilight of the Gods, that we've crept to the edge of eternity.

We are empiricists, chopping the root of the universe, all unaware that there can be an end until there is an end and we experience it.

Yggdrasil, say the Icelandic Sagas, is the wondrous tree that supports the universe. It is the world-tree.

Three roots has Yggdrasil; and for each root there is a spring, by which the tree is watered.

The Norns guard the spring, which is in Asgard, the dispensers of human fate, of whom there are also three: Urda, the Past; Verdandi, the Present; and Skuld, the Future.

A second root of Yggdrasil is watered by the spring of Wisdom, guarded by Mimir the Wise.

But the third root goes unguarded. It is forever being gnawed by the serpent Nidhogge, the Serpent of Darkness. One day he will bite right through the root, and Yggdrasil will fall, and the universe itself will fail.

That day is called Ragnarok, the Twilight of the Gods.

Shall there never come such a day? Oh, but there shall. It is coming soon.

But isn't the Icelandic myth false in fact? Perhaps it is; but its instinct and its perception are better than our own. It is a language, at least, with which to interpret meanings in the world. We see the surface only and think that the surface is all. We see words and think they are nothing but stones. We see an entire story and think it is nothing but a white oak tree. We see prophecy and can read nothing there but firewood and kindling.

Some myth is better than no myth at all. Myth is convinced that Deity is greater than the world and can bring it to an end, but that Deity persists in writing legends in the clay of the world until the end should come.

Myth could read the fall of an oak tree.

But Truth is best of all (though our contemporary notions of reality have difficulty distinguishing Truth from myth). Truth does more than read the beginning and the endings of oak trees. Truth embraces both. Truth is there at every beginning and every ending, even at the beginning and the ending of the world—which shall indeed have its ending.

For: *I am Alpha and Omega,* says Truth, *the beginning and the end, the first and the last.*

Christ is Truth, which brackets and signatures Time, with which to read the world and the fall of a white oak tree— before which, stand in awe.

The grace of our Lord Jesus Christ be with you all.

Amen.